Before, During and After the College of Your Dreams

Practical Advice from a Harvard Graduate

By

Paul J. Kim

ISBN: 1-4107-9093-2 (e-book)
ISBN: 1-4107-9092-4 (Paperback)

Library of Congress Control Number: 2003096966

This book is printed on acid free paper.

Printed in the United States of America
Bloomington, IN

1st Books - rev. 10/27/03

To my loving parents, Hyun Chul & Chung, for their selfless sacrifice and unflinching devotion to their sons. Our life in America is a gift from them. Our success in America is our gift to them.

A warm THANK YOU to the following folks who made me who I am today and helped to make this book possible:

- My beautiful wife Yuni, my stalwart brother David, my wonderful parents-in-law Clifford & Sun Cha;

- Cherished friends from the age of nostalgia: Alice, Esq., Angela, Dave Theodore, Dr. Esther, James, Esq., Dr. Kaytan, Nabil, Esq., Dr. Rebekah, Soo Jung and Dr. Steve & Emita;

- Dear friends at Ambassadors Presbyterian Church in Bound Brook, NJ where Yuni and I got married (www.ambassadorsministry.org) : Pastor Joe, Galen & Helen, JB & Jina, Pastor JP & Keren and Hwan & Shin;

- Loyal friends from business school and law school: Adam & Meltem, Alex, Andrew &

Maryanne, Dan & Sumi, Erik & Yumiko, John & Lily, Noraima, Steve & Joy and Dr. Will & Dr. Ping; and

- Esteemed teachers, mentors and colleagues over the years who were integral to my success: Anwar, Mr. Winokur, Dr. Kim, Esq., Gary, Haresh, Dr. Hyung Gu, Mr. DeSimone, Jen, Mrs. Herz, Keith, Mr. Sohn, Laura, Ms. Brooks, Nancy, Dr. Paul, Dr. Peter, Mr. Samek, Esq., Phil, Rick, Mr. Gong, Mr. Rodney, Mrs. Kornberg, Sam, "Hizzonah" Sandip, "Professor" Sanjay, Sebby, Mr. Abramsky, Mr. Magid, Mr. Lee, Esq., Mr. Chi, Tommy, Utpal, Professor Schroeder, Esq., Yolanda, Rev. Chang and the Yoshida family.

Table of Contents

I. Introduction

Paul J. Kim

1. Why should you read this book?

When a high school student visits the local bookstore, she can find numerous books dealing with the college admissions process. These include SAT prep materials, college profiles, personal essay guidebooks, application strategy manuals and even a collection of commentaries by admissions officers. In addition, there are private tutoring institutions throughout the country that provide assistance with standardized exam preparation, personal essay development and even admissions interview coaching. Indeed, an overabundance of resources is available to help her to gain admission to a competitive college.

But . . . what happens after she gets to the college of her dreams?

I recently read a New York City newspaper article entitled, "Does Gaining Admission to a Prestigious University Equal Prosperity?" (The Korea Daily, 6/21/03). With the aid of thought-provoking examples, the article implied that there does not necessarily seem to be a connection. These examples mentioned a frustrated mother whose son graduated from Harvard but could not find a job and ended up moving back in with his parents for a year. Unfortunately, there are many other graduates of competitive colleges who are in similar situations.

What went wrong? How could such promising young students work so diligently throughout high school to get into a prestigious university, spend four years studying at schools like Harvard, Duke or

Wellesley and end up graduating without a job (or a decent-paying job) or even plans for graduate school?

After much reflection, it is my opinion that these circumstances arise mainly because these individuals focused too much of their energies on getting into the prestigious schools and not enough time thinking about what they should accomplish during their college years and how they should accomplish it. I should know. I was one of these students.

From eight grade to twelfth grade, my sole purpose in life was to get into Harvard.

"If you get into Harvard, you are guaranteed a successful life!"

"Harvard educates the leaders of tomorrow. If you want to be a leader, and not a follower, you must go to Harvard."

These and other "words of wisdom" entranced me. I worked hard and made numerous sacrifices during my years at the highly selective Stuyvesant High School in New York City. As a result, I got into

Harvard University. In September 1990, I showed up at Harvard . . . CLUELESS about what I should do next. Within a month, I finally admitted to myself that I was lost at Harvard.

***

I wrote this book to provide practical advice on three critical issues:

1. How to get into a competitive college;
2. How to use one's time wisely while at top-tier school; and
3. How to develop one's long-term career upon graduating from a prestigious university.

These three issues combined form the actual overall challenge that confronts students (everyone from those in junior high school to those in college) and their parents. I have overcome this challenge over the past thirteen years and I want to impart to the readers how they can as well.

For convenience, I have laid out the content of this book in a question and answer format. In my responses to these questions, I also share various personal stories for illustrative purposes. These Q&A entries are based on numerous coaching sessions with consulting clients, friends, colleagues and of course, relatives. In addition, I make references to persons, organizations and literary sources which I believe add value to the discussions at hand. Please note, however, the contents of this book reflect only my personal views and not necessarily their views.

Furthermore, my advice is based on personal experiences and observations gathered through a "dual perspective." For example, I have seen the university admissions process over the past decade from the angle of a successful applicant as well as an alumni admissions interviewer for Harvard University and for Columbia Business School. In addition, I have developed a rewarding professional career working with prestigious Wall Street-caliber firms and Corporate American icons and have served actively on on-campus recruiting teams evaluating student candidates for employment.

***

Getting into a competitive college by itself is meaningless. A student has to do something productive with the opportunity in preparation for her future. This book is designed to help in this regard. Even though I would like to, I cannot make any guarantees of outcomes based on my advice. This is because each person's future is based on factors unique to each individual. However, all of the advice I present in this book is intended to influence the reader's odds of success in a positive way.

II. Getting into College: the Stuyvesant Years

Paul J. Kim

1. How did you select your classes?

I had two guiding principles in terms of choosing courses. The first principle –

Choose courses in which you feel confident that you can handle the subject matter covered in class.

The second principle –

Choose courses in which you feel comfortable with the instructor.

In light of these principles, let me qualify by saying that I was not an academic lightweight. My coursework was challenging. But then again, I was also a realist, a type of academic strategist. Basically, I was very selective about the battles that I fought –

I fought battles that I thought I could win.

Given that having an impressive Grade Point Average ("GPA") was extremely important for the college admissions success, I was not going to let my pride dictate which classes I took. Pride could potentially jeopardize my chances of achieving a high GPA and thus my chances of getting into a competitive school. I had a hard time understanding classmates who intentionally took required classes with the most harshly grading teachers. It was not as if I was going to learn less physics by taking the subject with a teacher who was a more flexible grader. At the end of the year, we all had to take the same statewide aptitude exam (the "Regents" exam). I performed as well as or even better than many of my classmates who took physics with "hard" teachers. I also walked away with a higher GPA.

I was a realist. I was not going to take classes that were going to add unnecessary stress to my academic schedule just so that I can show off to classmates how tough my schedule was. Knowing that I was not comfortable with science classes, I purposely avoided Advanced Placement ("AP") Physics, AP Chemistry and AP Biology. I did well in each of these subjects in the "regular" level classes offered to the general student body. I learned a great deal and enjoyed myself. But I also knew that I had a certain level of performance that I felt that I could not achieve if I took these subjects at a more advanced level. Thus I avoided these classes.

I pursued challenging classes that I felt I could manage. I took only three AP courses in while at Stuyvesant: AP Spanish, AP Macroeconomics and AP

Calculus (AB). In addition, I took Hebrew for two years. I realized that I had a preference for liberal arts classes. Hence, I focused my energies on liberal arts classes and did well. I felt no need to take classes that had intimidating course titles for the sake of impressing classmates or college admissions offices. Which is better? A 99 in a "regular" Chemistry class or a 90 in an AP Chemistry class? I would say the prior. If you can get a solid, mid-90s grade in the AP Chemistry class or higher, that is even better. But I was not sure I could achieve such a grade. Therefore, I focused on classes that seemed more manageable. For those of you who do not have confidence in liberal arts classes but rather in science or math classes, then I hope you will not take classes such as Hebrew just for the sake of taking the classes. As the old saying goes, "Don't bite off more than you can chew."

***

The other dimension of my class selection strategy was taking classes offered by teachers with whom I felt comfortable. Of course, I could not achieve this in all of my classes every semester. When I was stuck with teachers with whom I felt uncomfortable, I dealt with it the best that I could. I worked very hard and very diligently and achieved a great deal of success in classes offered by "difficult teachers." But when I had the ability to select my teachers, I chose to study under teachers who did not feel the need to intimidate students by being very harsh graders and by administering extremely difficult exams. I am of the mindset that you do not need to give extremely difficult exams in order to ensure that your students learn key lessons. One of my favorite teachers was my high school chemistry teacher, Mr. Rodney. He knew that his students would all have to take the Chemistry Regents Exam at the end of the school year. Thus, Mr.

15

Rodney geared his exams towards developing the basic competencies required to perform well on this upcoming exam. His tests were fair but also very thorough. I learned a great deal of chemistry in his class. I am very glad that I studied chemistry with him as opposed to another teacher who administered exams that were more difficult than they needed to be. At Stuyvesant, there were plenty of such teachers.

The above is based on the ability to change one's course schedule to fit with one's wishes. I was not able to do this all the time. However, I was able to alter my course schedule to a significant degree because of my extracurricular activities. Basically, as a member of the Boys' Swim Team and the Manager of the Girls' Swim Team, I needed to leave school early on certain days in order to get to competitions. With this argument, I lobbied many administrators and teachers so that I could make beneficial changes to my schedule each academic semester.

2. Why are extracurricular activities important? What is the ideal number of extracurricular activities for an applicant?

College is a comprehensive learning experience. In-class learning occurs for about fifteen hours per week. The university administration can manage the education of its students while the students are in class. Of greater importance to the administration is what its students will learn when not in class. Basically –

A college student spends about ninety percent of her time outside of a classroom – learning from and teaching fellow classmates in a variety of settings.

Hence, universities strive to create an environment wherein students will find themselves intellectually stimulated, particularly outside of the classroom.

The primary method of creating such an environment is by populating each entering class with students who have something to share with others –

Whether it is artistic talent, athleticism, political ideals, business ability or unique life experiences, a successful candidate must demonstrate to the admissions committee that she has attributes that are worthy of sharing with others.

A student can develop these attributes through her activities outside of class, in other words, high school extracurricular activities. How a student spends her time outside of class while in high school indicates what is important to her. What is important to her will command her passion. What she is passionate about, she will share with others, particularly in a college setting –

The more a student shares of herself with others, the more she will contribute to the university environment. This is the primary rationale of the admissions officers when evaluating students and their extracurricular activities.

The second rationale for the importance placed on extracurricular activities by admissions officers is that–

A student's level of involvement in extracurricular activities indicates her time management skills as well as commitment to an undertaken endeavor.

One of the most important skills to cultivate while in college is –

Time management – the ability to handle a multitude of important tasks simultaneously in a given amount of time.

College is a freewheeling environment wherein a student is solely responsible for how she spends her time. College admissions officers want to see that a student will not waste time but rather, spend time wisely and efficiently so that a student will make the most of her academic and non-academic experiences while at the institution.

In order to cultivate time-management skills, a student must possess some skills prior to arrival at college. Admissions committees detect time-management skills by evaluating a student's ability to manage a demanding academic workload as well as a diverse set of extracurricular activities during her high school career.

One of the ways in which college admissions officers are evaluated is by the attrition rate of an entering class during the four years in which they are at the university. Essentially, the fewer the students who drop out, the more successful an admissions committee was in selecting its entering class.

It is very embarrassing for any university to show that it selected for admission a noticeable number of students who had to drop out because they could not handle the time management challenges of college.

It is also a waste of the university's resources. A reliable source at Harvard once told me that a student's annual tuition only covers about half of what the university actually spends to educate each student. When a student leaves, the university does not recover the financial resources that it used for the student –

Paul J. Kim

Admissions officers interpret continuity and dedication to a specific set of extracurricular activities as an indication that a student is not going to quit and leave the university when things get difficult.

Colleges are more optimistic about students who find and stick with a set of activities for three or four years during high school rather than students who have a wide variety of one-year-involvement activities.

***

In terms of a student's collection of extracurricular activities –

There is no "ideal number" of extracurricular activities that the colleges require.

It is an individual issue that varies by applicant. However, I like to use the traditional American Thanksgiving Day Dinner as a model for designing one's extracurricular activities portfolio.

The traditional American Thanksgiving Day Dinner is one of the most elaborate culinary spreads that the average person in America will enjoy with her family. There are main entrées such as the turkey and perhaps some chicken and/or ham. There are a plethora of side dishes including corn, sweet potato, greens and cranberry sauce. Each person at the dinner table partakes of the meal as she pleases.

A hearty Thanksgiving Day Dinner usually entails a good portion of an entrée or two and a generous serving of a variety of side dishes. If a person's meal consisted only of turkey or only of side dishes, then the meal would be a bit odd to say the least.

This is how many college admissions committees view a candidate's portfolio of extracurricular activities. An entrée is a metaphor for a major extracurricular activity. A side dish represents a minor activity. (I will define these below.) In effect –

A high school student should have a diverse portfolio of major and minor extracurricular activities when applying to college, much like a hearty Thanksgiving Day Dinner.

3. What were your major extracurricular activities? How did you select these?

My major extracurricular activities were those in which I strove to achieve high levels of leadership responsibility and/or performance.

These included my high school swim team and my church youth group. Of these commitments, the more meaningful was my involvement with the Boys' Swim Team.

Prior to matriculating at Stuyvesant, I swam competitively and thus felt confident that I could find success on the high school swim team. With that in mind, I tried out for and made it onto the Stuyvesant High School Boys' Swim Team. I joined with the mindset that I was ultimately going to become one of the Co-Captains of the team. I dedicated myself to this goal. I rarely missed workouts or swim meets. At every opportunity, I swam with dedication and effort. I was not the most gifted swimmer. However, I was good enough to hold my own. For this, my coach rewarded me with a position in the starting line up during my first year on the Varsity Team. Throughout my four years on the team, I continued to develop into a solid swimmer. During my senior year, my hard work paid off. I was voted by my teammates as one of the Co-Captains of the team.

4. How did your extracurricular activities contribute to your high school experience?

My involvement with the swim team provided me with invaluable lessons and life-altering experiences during high school. First –

My swim team experiences taught me valuable lessons in time management.

In addition to my academics, I could count on swimming to be the other key component of my high school years. Basically, my days were not going to be focused solely on academics. I would have to balance my time and energies between my books and the pool.

Try swimming five thousand yards (nearly three miles) in a period of about two hours. Then commute back home on public transportation for an hour and a half, all after a full day of school. By the time you get home around 7:30pm, I guarantee that you will be extremely tired. But you cannot go to bed or relax in front of the television. This is because you have a full load of homework (usually 4 subjects or so) and usually an exam or two for which you need to prepare. Not to mention the need to eat dinner. That was my time management challenge during my four years in high school.

Under such circumstances, I prioritized my activities and became extremely, extremely efficient with my homework assignments, exam preparation and report writing. I could not afford not to be that way.

I needed to maximize the usage of every minute of every day. This entailed studying for exams, completing reading assignments and doing problem sets on trains, ferries and buses.

Also, during swim meets, when I was not competing or warming up, I was doing my homework in the stands that were reserved for spectators. I did my best to use my time productively and not waste it. My daily goal was to have the minimum amount of homework to complete at home by the time I returned home. My long-term goal was to achieve and maintain the highest grade point average possible. All the while, I also aimed to be the best swimmer I could be.

***

In addition –

Paul J. Kim

The swim team gave me a tremendous sense of friendship and camaraderie.

I felt as though I fit in with a reliable group of individuals with whom I shared a meaningful common bond. What was that common bond? It was the everyday physical struggle to develop our swimming abilities. Swimming was a great equalizer. Our team had rich white kids from the Upper West Side of Manhattan, Eastern European immigrant kids from Brooklyn, math geeks, history buffs, kids from the popular hang out crowds, etc. No matter who you were in the hallways and classrooms, when you came to swim, you were a swimmer. All of us were swimmers. This meant that each person was evaluated by his efforts in the pool and his dedication to the swim team. Popularity and respect on the team did not come from pure swimming ability. Rather, they developed over time due to an individual's hard work and dedication towards the common cause of team victory.

When you swim together, hang out in the locker room together, travel to competitions together, win together, lose together and travel home together for five months straight each academic year, you cannot help but develop deep friendships.

To this day, one of my closest friends is a fellow swimmer from Stuyvesant.

Steve and I met during our freshman year during a conversation when we discovered that we both intended to try out for the swim team. Both of us made it onto the team. Afterwards, we swam together for four years and both were selected as Co-Captains by our teammates. While we were in college, we stayed in touch, seeing each other every time we were back in NYC from our respective colleges for holiday and summer break. After we graduated from college, I went to Korea to work and Steve returned to NYC to attend medical school. Despite the geographical distance, we still kept in touch and whenever I returned to NYC, we always met and shared meals together over nostalgic conversations as well as discussions about our future aspirations.

Shortly after I returned to NYC from Korea, Steve got married. I was one of his groomsmen. Then it was his turn to move away. He went to Los Angeles to start his career as a physician with a prestigious medical residency program at the UCLA Medical Center. We always met when he returned periodically to NYC to visit his family. Later, when I joined Johnson & Johnson and went on business trips to Los Angeles, we would spend time together. Sometimes, he and his wife Emita traveled to my hotel for dinner. Sometimes, I drove to his home. By the way, Steve and Emita also met in a swim team environment when they were in junior high school. This past year,

Steve stood with me as one of my groomsmen when I married my beautiful wife and kindred spirit Yuni.

Without the bonding experience provided by the Stuyvesant High School Boys' Swim Team, I would never have had the opportunity to develop such a close friendship with a person such as Steve. Throughout high school, we had only one class together (a semester of Physics) and had no other extracurricular activities in common. The swim team was the sole reason why we became friends.

***

In addition to the friendship and camaraderie –

During my four years of swimming, I developed a great deal of perseverance and strength of purpose.

Mr. DeSimone's (our coach) daily workouts were demanding. Our team was probably one of the hardest training teams among all of the public and private high school swim teams in New York City. Mr. DeSimone was serious about swimming and as a result, his swimmers shared his outlook. This also translated into strong efforts in the pool.

Mr. DeSimone always pushed me to my limits. As a freshman, I wanted to swim easier events such as the 100-yard freestyle. However, Mr. D (a nickname which he acquired during his early days of coaching) had other plans. He assigned me to the 100-yard butterfly. The butterfly was not an easy stroke. It took a great deal of endurance to swim this event at every swim meet during the year, but I got through it. During my sophomore year, as I became more and more comfortable with this event, Mr. D pushed me further by assigning me to the 200-yard individual medley (an event in which I had to swim eight laps – two laps of each respective stroke: butterfly, backstroke, breaststroke and freestyle) and the 500-yard freestyle (an endurance event requiring 20 continuous laps). The 100-yard butterfly, the 200-yard individual medley and the 500-yard freestyle events are considered to be the most challenging individual events during a swim meet. Mr. D had me train for and swim at least two of these three events at each swim meet during my sophomore, junior and senior years.

There was one memorable swim meet wherein I swam the 500-yard freestyle event. During my sophomore year, Stuyvesant swam against Brooklyn Technical High School ("Brooklyn Tech") for the bronze medal in the City Championships. I was pitted against a swimmer who seemed to tower over me in height and reach.

In most 500-yard freestyle events, a clear winner emerges within the first six laps because someone pulls away from the pack early on in the race and maintains a significant lead for the remainder of the event. This 500-yard freestyle event was different. The lead swimmer from Brooklyn Tech and I swam at a virtually identical pace for the first eighteen laps of the race. I had never encountered a swimmer who pushed me so hard. I did not want to relinquish the lead. Neither did he.

As I took breaths while taking every other stroke, I saw that both teams were extremely excited about the race. Everyone was on his feet. At lap nineteen, I gained the lead for good. But at a cost. When I finished the race, I was completely exhausted. I could not climb out of the pool with my own strength. My teammates literally had to pull me out. I lay on the pool deck until I regained my strength several minutes later. During that time, Mr. D came over and gave me a hug and congratulated me.

I learned a key lesson from this experience. I learned that –

My mind could master my body.

During the race, my body was telling me to give up and let my competitor win. He was bigger and faster. Just to keep up with him, my body had to work overtime. Therefore, my body kept rebelling. My mind, however, did not agree. My mind was firmly made up. I was not going to lose. I saw that I could keep up with my competitor with about 95% of my efforts. I kept saving up the last 5% of effort from each lap until the last two laps when I gave it my final push. Essentially, my mind disciplined my body and forced it to follow the goal that my mind had set.

This was a pivotal moment for me during my high school career. After a year and a half, I began to feel the physical strain of commuting nearly three hours daily and actively participating in several hours of extracurricular activities per week. Not to mention the academics. My body was becoming weary. This 500-yard freestyle event taught me that if my mind told my body to follow, it would. After this event, my body did not complain about the physical demands of my high school experience. My mind did not allow it to do so because there were too many important goals to reach throughout high school.

5. What were your minor extracurricular activities? How did you select these?

My minor extracurricular activities were those that served as filler activities that took the place of my major activities when the major activities had not begun yet or were completed for the academic year.

I had a large number of minor activities, in a great variety of areas. To name a few: Big Sibling, Christian Club, SING (a competitive theatrical competition), Student Government (Class Senator, Student Union Executive Committee) and the school newspaper.

My goal with minor activities was to demonstrate to the colleges that I can manage diverse challenges and that I was not going to rest on my swimming laurels.

Among these, I found the most personal reward as a Big Sibling. The Big Sibling program at Stuyvesant assigned juniors and seniors to homeroom classes of entering students. The older students were charged with providing mentorship to the younger students. As a "Big Sib," I appreciated the opportunity to share with my younger schoolmates the lessons that I learned during my time at Stuyvesant. Helping students to handle Stuyvesant 's administrative issues, select extracurricular activities and learn about various academic programs provided me with a great sense of satisfaction that I was improving others' high school experiences.

6. How did you prepare for your SAT and other college entrance examinations? Which SAT II and Advanced Placement Tests did you take?

I was very nervous about my standardized exams. Having secured a high GPA, I was focused on achieving commensurate standardized examination results. With that in mind, I invested a great deal of time and energy to this goal.

For my SATs, I studied at a local Asian community prep school (CCB English School – the same school that prepared

41

*me for the Stuyvesant High School Entrance Examination)
and at a mainstream, nationwide test prep center. Honestly,
I think I gained much more at CCB.*

I spent the summer between my sophomore and junior years studying at CCB. Everyday, I went to CCB and drilled on math problems and verbal problems. The rigor and discipline gained from CCB helped me a great deal. The mainstream test prep center taught more by emphasizing pattern recognition and short cuts. Sometimes these work. However –

*When you encounter the difficult level questions on the
SAT, you need to know how to solve the problems, not be an
expert on short cuts.*

CCB taught me the fundamental math and verbal skills that I needed when taking the SAT.

Unfortunately, I did not realize this quickly enough.

***

I enrolled in a pair of classes at the same mainstream test prep center for my SAT II Tests on English (Writing) and Math IIc and spent (or should I say "wasted"?) a great deal of money.

Attending the mainstream test prep center was the popular thing to do among my classmates. I should have studied on my own, as I did for my SAT II Physics exam. I was the type of person who learned the fundamentals of a topic with more ease than the fancy tricks and shortcuts. Ultimately, I performed well enough on these exams for my college choices to smile on me. However, I should have trusted my instincts about my studying style and not given into the social pressure to study in a certain way or with a certain school.

***

Although I took three AP classes (Spanish, Calculus AB and Macroeconomics), I did not take any AP Exams.

But I wish I had. I should have applied myself a bit more each year so that I could have been prepared to take the exams. Perhaps if I had taken enough AP courses and exams, I could have been done with college in three years, rather than four. Perhaps not? Regardless of my thoughts on something I cannot change, I will recommend that if you are able to sit for AP Exams, take as many as you can. You never know . . . you might be able to save a lot of money in the long run.

7. How did you spend each summer vacation and why?

I selected each of my summer vacation activities because I felt that these would contribute directly or indirectly towards the realization of my goal of getting into Harvard.

In other words, I chose activities that were going to help me get into a competitive college.

After my freshman year, I spent the summer at a YMCA swimming clinic and camp in order to improve my swimming skills.

45

By doing this, I would be an even better contributor to my swim team. This would enable me to be in a better position to be considered for a Co-Captain spot in the future. Being a Co-Captain would help my extracurricular activities stand out when I applied for college. That was my logic behind selecting this activity.

This activity was of special meaning to me because I had an opportunity to swim with my old swim coach, Nancy. During junior high school, I swam competitively with her team at the Flushing YMCA. This is the environment where I first developed my skills as a competitive swimmer. This is where I "paid my dues." Upon matriculating at Stuyvesant, I had to quit the YMCA team due to my school schedule. It was very good to return to my old coach and swim under her tutelage. She was a coach who emphasized the fundamentals. I learned a great deal from her and developed into a much stronger swimmer – one with greater speed and endurance.

***

After my sophomore year, I attended CCB English School's summer session in order to prepare for my SATs.

SATs, SATs, SATs. This was the big exam for getting into college. I had to do well. Nothing intimidated me as much as this exam. I was going to do whatever I could to achieve success on this exam, including dedicating an entire summer vacation.

***

The summer before my senior year, I participated in a summer study program at Georgetown University.

It was an academic program at the university where I could take college-level courses with other high school students. My reasoning was that I needed to prove to the colleges to which I planned to apply that I could do well in college-level academics. What better way to do this than to study at a prestigious university and do well academically?

I wanted to attend Harvard Summer School. But this was not an option. My parents were of limited financial resources. We could not afford the tuition required to attend any of the Ivy League summer programs such as Harvard, Yale, Brown, Cornell, etc. So –

I did some bargain hunting to find a summer program at a prestigious university for an affordable price.

After some deliberation, I chose to apply to Georgetown.

Georgetown was a great experience. I took a class on International Relations. It was my first exposure to college academics. At first, I was not used to the lengthy reading assignments. I fell behind my classmates very quickly. As a result, my mid-term exam results were not pleasing. However, I learned my lesson for the second half of the summer term and buckled down with my studying. I did very well on the final exam and walked away from the class with a strong grade. I proved to myself and to my future college targets that I could achieve success in the academic environment of a competitive college.

Paul J. Kim

8. Did you have a part-time job or a summer job? Why did you select these jobs?

I never held a part-time or a summer job throughout high school. Please do not interpret my not having held a part-time or summer job as a value judgment on my part that it is not worthwhile. I was too involved with my extracurricular activities at school as well as my summer activities to engage in a part-time or summer job.

But had I not been as busy, I definitely would have looked for part-time or summer jobs in which I could learn the importance of managing money and about the realities of the world.

There are a plethora of different types of part-time and summer jobs available to high school students. These include service jobs (i.e., waiting on tables, delivery jobs), analytical jobs (i.e., bank/corporate intern, office clerk), sales jobs (i.e., retail sales), and manual labor (i.e., construction, farm hand, factory production). Regardless of the job that a person selects, she must learn the importance of managing money and the realities of the world not taught in school.

With respect to the importance of managing money, there is a saying that "Money makes the world go around."

Regardless of how much education you have, no matter where you live, irrespective of your occupation, MONEY is absolutely necessary in order to pay for food, clothing and shelter. MONEY is a powerful force that impacts every single aspect of life.

If you do not take control of your money and learn to make it work for you, it will control you and you will work for it – basically, you will end up in a bad situation.

If you mismanage your money, it is likely that your financial credit will suffer, or worse, you will go broke. If you have bad financial credit, then you will face significant obstacles when you want to undertake even the most basic of life's "grown up" activities such as buying a car or getting a mortgage to purchase a home. Banks will not lend to those who have bad credit.

How do banks define those with bad credit? Essentially, people who do not have personal assets (possessions of significant value – such as a car, land, stocks, bonds, etc. – which can be converted into cash, if necessary, to cover financial obligations) or people who have a track record of not paying their bills in a timely manner (either because they did not have money or because they lacked the discipline required to meet these financial obligations). These days, it is not unusual for employers to conduct credit checks on potential employees to make sure that they pay their bills on time. The logic is that if the person maintains a good financial credit record through responsible behavior, then she will be a reliable employee. The fundamental lesson is that –

You need to save money, invest in personal assets and pay your bills on time.

Regarding the realities of the world, there is a saying that "You cannot eat prestige." A funny statement, but a profound one. It means that –

A person's impressive educational background by itself will not provide her with a good-paying job. Her impressive pedigree must be accompanied by comparable skills that will enable her to earn money.

So far, my experiences have been the following. Having a Harvard degree helped me to secure interviews for great jobs. But once I got these interviews, I had to convince my potential employers that I had the skills they required of employees. Furthermore, once I began at my new job, I had to perform to the best of my ability and meet or exceed my employers' expectations so that I still had my job the next day.

A prestigious background may create job opportunities, but only a person's skills and work ethic will enable her to capitalize on those opportunities.

When an employer considers a person with a prestigious educational background for a job, that employer is like a car shopper who considers buying a BMW. The buyer will have high expectations of a BMW, for instance, that it will be a better performing car than your average Ford Escort. In the same way, an employer who considers hiring a Harvard graduate will expect the person to be a higher caliber employee than someone without such a prestigious background.

If the BMW does not live up to the driver's expectations, then the driver will return it to the dealer and ultimately get rid of the car.

In the same way, a Harvard graduate must perform, or else, she will be fired. What is the basic lesson? Regardless of where you attend school and what you study, make sure that you develop skills that will enable you to perform well in your chosen profession. Or else, you will go hungry. Prestige and pedigree in and of themselves will not put food on the table.

Paul J. Kim

9. Who wrote your college recommendations? How did you select these individuals? How did you approach them for recommendations?

I received three academic recommendations and three non-academic recommendations.

My academic recommendations were from teachers who taught me a diverse set of disciplines. I wanted to demonstrate to the admissions committees that I could succeed in a wide variety of subject matters. The non-

academic recommendations were from those who oversaw my key extracurricular activities.

Mr. Abramsky was my social studies (American Government) teacher. He reminded me of a scholarly professor who held his students to a higher degree of expectations. But definitely not in a strict way. He engaged us in conversation during class in a manner where he naturally lifted our intellectual performance to a higher level. It was in a way such that I wanted to perform better and better. Hence, I prepared more diligently for his class than for any other class. This led to casual conversations outside of class that led to a strong rapport.

Mrs. Kornberg was my foreign language teacher. Namely, she taught me Spanish for one year and Hebrew for two years. She was a kind-hearted and dedicated teacher who showed great interest in my life outside of the classroom. I shared with her my triumphs in the swimming pool and in other classes.

After Mom, Mrs. Kornberg was my key mother figure during high school.

Mr. Winokur was my teacher for two math classes - Pre-Calculus and Linear Algebra - and my homeroom teacher for one year. He had an easy-going personality thus, his classroom was low stress. I thrived in this environment. I generally did not perform as well in math classes compared to history or language classes. But in Mr. Winokur's class, I felt uninhibited because he had a welcoming ambience. With this, I found myself speaking out more and more in his class and as a result, doing very well on his examinations.

Aside from my desire to select teachers who taught diverse, core academic subjects, I chose to ask these teachers for recommendations because I had a good relationship with them. The good relationship was based on two key factors: 1. I performed well in their class; and 2. I maintained a conversational relationship with them even after I had completed their classes.

It is easier to ask a friend for a favor than it is to ask someone with whom you do not have a relationship. Given my close relationship with these teachers, I brought the topic up during the course of my regular conversations with them.

With Mrs. Kornberg, for example, I brought it up during a conversation about an upcoming swimming meet. With Mr. Winokur, I brought up the topic during homeroom. With Mr. Abramsky, I approached the topic during a hallway conversation. I did not make appointments or take any extraordinary steps. It was a natural offshoot of my relationship with each of them.

***

In addition to my teachers, I also received recommendations from my Stuyvesant High School swim team coach, my church pastor and the Consul General of the Korean consulate of New York City.

Next to Dad, Mr. DeSimone was the single most influential adult-male figure during my high school years. He was a role model for all of us on the swim team. I met Mr. D, as we called him, during the tryouts for the boys' swim team during my freshman year back in 1986. He was a dedicated and caring leader of Stuyvesant's boys' and girls' swim teams. He lived in Suffolk County and traveled several hours a day to give the boys' and girls' teams the guidance we needed to capture several championship titles. During my high school years, he saw me grow up from an inexperienced freshman starter on the varsity team to a confident Co-Captain of a Division Champion team during my senior year. He knew of my dedication to the swim team and to my academics. Every semester, Mr. D reviewed each swimmer's report card to determine if the swimmer was academically eligible to swim. If a swimmer did not maintain a certain GPA, the swimmer was not allowed to compete, according to Stuyvesant High School's rules and regulations.

Given my close relationship to Mr. D, it was very natural for me to ask him for a recommendation. I approached him after a workout, prior to heading into the locker room to shower and change into my street clothes.

He was very happy to write a college recommendation for me. He asked me which school I hoped to attend. I told him Harvard. He smiled and said, "I am not surprised." A week later, he told me he was done with my recommendation letter.

I also asked my church pastor, Reverend Chang, for a recommendation. I had attended the Korean-American Presbyterian Church of Queens since fourth grade. He knew my involvement in the church youth group. Reverend Chang was a very generous and good-hearted spiritual advisor to his congregation. He prayed for me in his office, one on one, each time I embarked upon a milestone academic event: the Stuyvesant High School entrance examination when I was in eighth grade, the SAT and SAT II examinations, etc. I found much courage as a result of his prayers. In light of Korean cultural norms, my parents asked him for a college recommendation on my behalf. He was more than happy to provide me with one. He referred to my active involvement in the church as well as provided a solid character reference. My family and I remain indebted to him.

Lastly, I received a recommendation from the Consul General of the Korean Consulate of New York City. I had never met Mr. Gong before. However, Mom knew him and his staff. At the time, Mom worked at the Park Avenue Branch of the Korea Exchange Bank. It was located in the same building as the Korean Consulate. Over time, she became friends with the staff at the Consulate and eventually became acquainted with the Consul General. During the course of the relationship, they became familiar with our family, including my brother David's and my endeavors at Stuyvesant High School. She did not know at the time that this relationship would eventually become helpful to her son's college application.

After I had submitted my college applications in late December of 1989, Mom decided to approach the Consul General for a recommendation on my behalf. Mom and Dad wanted to do everything possible to enhance my chances. Mr. Gong agreed. However, he wanted to know more about my candidacy for college. Hence, my parents drove out in the middle of the night to a remote retreat center (where I was with my church youth group for a winter retreat), drove me home so that I could prepare a brief autobiographical document, and then returned me to the retreat center the same night. Needless to say, it was a sleepless yet very productive evening for all. I was grateful for my parents' efforts. But most of all, I was grateful for Mr. Gong's recommendation letter.

10. How did you prepare for your college interviews?

A college interview is extremely important because this is the stage of the application process where the representatives of the respective colleges actually meet a student face to face and make first-hand assessments about her candidacy.

Everything in an application is either the student saying something about herself or someone else serving as her advocate. This, obviously, could lead to bias. The college admissions interview is a school's way to eliminate that bias and make its own judgment about the type of person the student is and whether or not the student is a good choice for the school.

As for my interviews, I had two on-campus interviews (Harvard and Columbia) as well as several alumni interviews (Harvard, Yale, MIT, UPenn and Georgetown). Yes, I interviewed with Harvard both on-campus and with an alumni. Harvard allowed candidates to have both types of interviews. Therefore,

I requested and received two opportunities to interview with Harvard.

The colleges stated that there is no difference between an alumni interview and an on-campus interview in terms of impact on a candidate's chances of admission. Nevertheless,

Before, During and After the College of Your Dreams

I wanted to demonstrate my desire to attend Harvard as much as possible. Hence, I traveled up to Cambridge, Massachusetts and visited the Harvard admissions office in November of 1989.

I interviewed with a member of the admissions staff. Subsequently, I had an alumni interview at the Harvard Club of New York.

***

I do not recall the exact details of my interviews. However –

As a current alumni admissions interviewer for Harvard University, I do have some comments on what I look for in candidates whom I assess.

Paul J. Kim

My comments are based on almost ten years of interviewing candidates in New York City, suburban New Jersey and Seoul, Korea.

First, the candidate should exercise basic "common sense."

The candidate should come dressed appropriately. Men should wear a suit. Women should wear something comparable. No matter what the occasion (a job interview or a college admissions interview), an interview is a serious matter. The candidate should present herself in the best manner possible. Also, the candidate should not use profanity during the interview, no matter how excited the candidate is about the topic of conversation. Harvard classes require many discussion sessions. Speaking in profanity is not welcome during those sessions and neither is it welcome during my interviews.

Second, the candidate should be able to express in a short,
intelligent manner, why she would like to attend the
university for which she is interviewing at the moment.

If the candidate's only reason for wanting to attend Harvard is its prestige, I usually become unimpressed. There are plenty of other schools that have stellar reputations. I want to know whether or not the candidate is familiar with the resources available to students at Harvard. For example, are there certain academic courses of study or exchange programs that interest the candidate? Are there any extracurricular activities that attract the candidate? Are there any other aspects of the university that capture the interest of the candidate? If a student knows of the resources that differentiate Harvard from other universities, then it is more likely that the student will use those resources during her time at Harvard and therefore have a more successful time while at the university. A candidate's familiarity with the university's offerings also demonstrates to me that the candidate is proactive. In other words, when the candidate faces challenges in life, she will take action to prepare herself to overcome those challenges. The Harvard experience will most likely present numerous challenges - personal, academic, extracurricular and professional. A strong desire to overcome such obstacles and to stretch oneself most certainly will come in handy during a student's years at Harvard.

Third, the candidate should be able to express the reasons why she is different and unique from other candidates.

Harvard's annual admissions rate is roughly 10%. This means that for every ten candidates who apply, only one gets admitted. Complicating matters further is that the vast majority of the competing students are those with extraordinary high school credentials. They are valedictorians of their graduating class. They are school/class presidents. They are nationally recognized athletes. They are top-rate research scholars. They are world-class musicians, actors and artists. They are a formidable group of individuals, all competing to get into Harvard.

As such, each candidate needs to "market" herself to the university and show why she is more unique among the candidate pool than others. This can be done through the admissions essay. However, the admissions interview is also a great opportunity to do so.

I look for students who demonstrate a certain passion for a specific extracurricular or academic pursuit that they can share with their classmates at Harvard.

Everyone has a different passion. For example, if a candidate is a can of paint and the entering class selected by the admissions committee is a portrait, the candidate's passion for a select endeavor is her paint color. Beautiful portraits are made with beautiful colors. The more passionate the candidate is about some endeavor, the more unique and beautiful her color will be. The more unique and beautiful her color, the more likely it is that she will be considered for inclusion in the entering class.

Fourth, the candidate should be self-aware and understand how others view her.

Roughly 90% of a student's time at Harvard will be spent outside of the classroom. That means that a student will teach and learn from others 90% of the time while in college. In order to make everyone's experience enjoyable and worthwhile, I look for candidates who are aware of how they impact others and how others view them. The question I ask of all of my candidates is the following –

"If your friends and family had to describe you with three adjectives, what would they be? Provide examples as to why you chose those adjectives."

If I do not receive a thoughtful answer, then the candidate's prospects are not positive. A candidate should be conscious of one's interactions with others. There will be countless interactions at Harvard at academic, social, personal and even professional levels. A candidate should be prepared for these.

Fifth, the candidate should be able to carry on an intelligent conversation about a diverse range of topics, including current events.

The vast majority of classes at Harvard are conducted in seminar/discussion style. This means that each candidate is expected to contribute meaningfully to the on-going discourse day in and day out. Therefore, I consider whether a candidate can converse at a reasonable level about different topics. I usually let the candidate choose the topic. But sometimes, I pick a popular topic and engage the candidate. This helps me to assess whether the candidate has the flexibility and capability to handle herself.

Sixth, the candidate should be able to pass the "roommate" test.

In college, a student is most likely to have an experience living with another person, whether in a dorm or in a shared apartment. Harvard strongly prefers to have all of its students live on campus. I had great roommates in college. I lived with Nabil and James for all four years. Nabil even stood as a groomsman at my wedding. My roommates made my college experience extremely pleasant and memorable. But not all roommate experiences are positive. I have seen terrible situations occur because people just did not get along. Although "it takes two hands to clap," I find that "one hand usually moves first." During my interviews, I try to see if the candidate would be a difficult roommate.

Is this person courteous? Is this person arrogant and inconsiderate of others' feelings? Does this person exercise a reasonable level of personal cleanliness? Is this person someone with whom I could have a meaningful personal chat in the late hours of the evening?

A student at Harvard faces enough challenges in the classroom and in extracurricular settings. She should not have to deal with challenges back "home" at the dormitory as well.

Seventh, the candidate should follow up promptly with a thank you note.

All interviewers volunteer their time to get to know candidates and possibly serve as the candidates' advocates to the admissions office. Candidates should express gratitude for interviewers' time and effort.

I have met a number of candidates regarding whom I was "on the fence."

I needed more time to determine whether or not I supported their candidacy for Harvard. A few of them sent thank you notes. A few of them did not.

The ones who sent thank you notes usually got a more positive assessment than had they not sent a thank you note at all.

By the way, a thank you note should be sent after any interview, whether it is for college admissions or for job applications.

11. Is it important to visit colleges? When should a student visit colleges?

It is absolutely important to visit colleges to which one plans to apply. Unless a candidate visits a school, how can a candidate know if she will enjoy spending four years at the school?

The candidate should visit colleges, if possible, and consider whether she likes the overall atmosphere of the school, the location of the school, the surrounding community and even the architectural style of the school. Furthermore, the candidate should sit in on some classes and talk to current students to get a feel for the day-to-day aspects of the school. This is the proverbial "kicking the tires" test.

Furthermore, as an alumni admissions interviewer, I regularly ask if the candidate has visited Harvard. If the candidate truly has a deep interest in the school, I expect her to have made the effort to see the school first-hand and furthermore, be able to share her impressions about the campus (whether positive or negative) with me during the interview.

Indeed, not everyone is able to make campus visits. However, I like to see that the candidate has made the effort. I am not alone among interviewers on this issue.

If at all possible, candidates should visit the schools to which they plan to apply.

Most students visit colleges during their junior or senior year. In my opinion –

There is no best time to visit. The key is that a candidate makes the effort to visit the schools within a reasonable timeframe prior to applying.

Paul J. Kim

12. What were your college essay topics? Do you have any tips on how to write these essays?

When I applied to college, different schools had their own essay requirements based on topics and length. I recall two essays. One asked for a page from my autobiography. The other was a general topic requirement, one that asked the applicant to select the topic.

For the first essay, I wrote a piece that demonstrated my passion for competitive swimming.

It was set in a swim meet where I competed in different events. I took the reader through the mental process that I underwent for each event: the preparation, launch and struggle to gain dominance and maintain the lead until the end. It was a glimpse into the grassroots struggles of a competitive swimmer and his sacrifices and desire to win.

My other essay dealt with academic integrity.

A critical observation about Stuyvesant was that there were many temptations and opportunities to cheat on exams, cut classes and plagiarize homework assignments. For four years, I saw many students engage rampantly in this sort of misbehavior. My greatest concern was that many of these students achieved high grades along with those of us who were faithful to our academic responsibilities.

My outrage was greater than that of the average student. I achieved my grades by diligently working on my academics and at the same time, managing my challenging extracurricular activities schedule. I expressed my desire to attend a university where a lack of academic integrity will not be tolerated. As I reflect on my classmates from high school, I still recall those who lacked academic integrity. Within my data set, it is very interesting that those who lacked academic integrity were those who also lacked social integrity.

***

In terms of writing essays, a student should approach it as an exercise in identifying her unique points and highlighting how these are in line with the characteristics of the target university.

What do I mean by this? When the admissions officers review student files, it is fairly certain that they will receive numerous applications from students with top GPAs, solid extracurricular activities and glowing recommendations. These documents only tell them ABOUT the student.

The essay is a method by which the admissions office hears DIRECTLY from the student. The essay will convey the student's candidacy in the student's own voice.

To do this effectively, the student must write an essay that will help to differentiate him/her from the myriad of other students who have similar profiles (academic, extracurricular, etc.). Each of us is an individual who can make a lasting and unique impression on the admissions office. A student should approach college essays in a manner that conveys to the admissions office what makes her unique and memorable and how the student and the university will both benefit by having the student attend.

Paul J. Kim

13. Did you apply early?

I did not apply early to any college. I was not ready
with my standardized exams until after the November
deadlines for early applications. Whether I would
have or not applied early, I do not know.

Applying early has its benefits as well as its
concerns. There are two ways that students normally
apply "early." Both of these processes require
applications to be sent in by November 1st (or the
designated date of a particular school). Both of these
methods result in a reply by Christmas time. The
difference between these two methods lies in what is

expected of the student if she receives an admission. The first method is called Early Admission.

Under Early Admission, the student has the option to decline the offer of admission and matriculate at another college.

The second method is called Early Decision. As its name suggests, a student is obligated to attend the particular college because the student has <u>decided</u> early on where she wants to attend college.

Applying early has its benefits.

Harvard's annual admissions rate is about 10%. Among early applicants, the rate improves to about 16% - 20%. Remember, about 20,000 students apply and about 2,000 are admitted each year. In recent years, about 5,000 – 6,000 students have applied early each year, with about 1,000 or so being admitted. Wait a minute. Does that mean Harvard selects roughly 50% of its successful candidates by Christmas time? Yes. Shouldn't a perspective candidate apply early? Not necessarily.

Applying early has its concerns, too.

The students who apply early are generally the best of the best. They are the students who have stronger potential for admission whether they apply early or with the regular schedule. As a result, competition is extremely difficult. If a candidate has a weakness or two in her application (for example, a less-than-stellar SAT score), the weakness will become even more conspicuous when compared to students who regularly score above 1500. Of course, early applicants who are not accepted can be deferred to the regular round instead of being rejected.

"Deferred" means that the admissions office will hold off on making a decision about the student until it has an opportunity to evaluate the student compared to the rest of the applicants.

Although the student will be evaluated fairly, she is fighting an up-hill battle. If I were an admissions officer who has to review a deferred student's application again, my basic question would be, "This candidate was not good enough to get admitted the first time we evaluated her. What is so special about this person compared to the candidates in the regular applicant pool?" The admissions office begins the second evaluation of the deferred candidate with a negative impression. Therefore, it stands to reason that a deferred student faces a more difficult challenge with the admissions committee than a student who applied on the regular schedule.

14. To which schools did you apply? Did you get into the schools of your choice?

I applied to the following colleges. "Dream Schools" - Harvard University and Yale University. "Mid-range Schools" - Massachusetts Institute of Technology, University of Pennsylvania (Wharton and Engineering dual degree program) and Columbia University. "Safety Schools" - Georgetown University and four State University of New York schools (Binghamton, Geneseo, Buffalo and Albany).

I gained admission to all of the schools above except Yale.

Paul J. Kim

15. If you could have done anything differently, what would it be? Why?

I consider my high school years to be extremely successful in every dimension. I did well in school. I had good friends. My family relationships were solid. I stayed out of trouble. Most of all, I was admitted to my top college choice.

With that in mind, if I had to change anything about my high school experience, perhaps it is the following.

Paul J. Kim

During my senior year at Stuyvesant, I should have pursued college scholarship programs more aggressively.

I do not know if I could have won any of these. However, if I did, I would have alleviated my parents' financial burden as they sent me to Harvard. The College Office at Stuyvesant regularly posted notices about scholarships. However, I, for some reason, call it laziness, apathy or lack of understanding, did not follow up with these opportunities and pursue them. I do have many regrets about this. I definitely should have been more in tune with these opportunities and capitalized on them. If not for me, then for my parents who paid for my Harvard tuition by selling our house in a "nice" neighborhood and downgrading to a small apartment in a "working-class" neighborhood.

III. What I ACTUALLY Learned at Harvard

Paul J. Kim

1. You reached your goal of getting into Harvard. Now what? What were your toughest challenges at Harvard? How did you overcome them?

For half a decade, getting into Harvard was my sole purpose and motivation for almost everything that I did.

As I reflect back on my youth, I realize that I was so fixated on accomplishing this goal of getting into Harvard that I never took the time to consider meaningfully what I would do once I got there.

Essentially, I fought and fought to get a chance to study at a prestigious university. Unfortunately, I did not give sufficient thought to the most critical issue of what it meant to attend a school such as Harvard.

In September of 1990, just after my parents left me in Cambridge, Massachusetts –

I came to the frightening realization that for the first time in many years, I did not have a life goal to pursue. I had no direction. I had no focus. I was lost.

What made it worse was that there were so many intelligent and diligent classmates around me who seemed to know what they wanted to do with their lives. I felt like I was being left behind. Being alone and feeling lost, I had a growing sense of fear and frustration. My fear was based on not knowing what I should do to fix the situation.

My frustration was based on my lack of ability to identify my goals early on and take decisive action and not waste time.

In the mean time, my academics began to suffer. During my first term, I took classes on microeconomics, anthropology/archaeology, Japanese history and Spanish.

I took this random assortment of classes because I did not know what I truly wanted to study in college.

My academic advisor encouraged me to "explore" and "see what it's like" to study certain topics. I'm sure it was not her intent but she worsened my situation by diffusing whatever focus I had left. Consequently, my grades began to falter. On my first midterm examination at Harvard, I got a "D." It was not a "D" for "delightful." Rather, I think it was a "D" for "dummy."

Drastic times called for drastic measures. I was so lost during my first semester that I did not grant myself the leeway to engage in any extracurricular activities. I was certain that my academic ship was sinking. Hence, I had to jettison everything that was not critical to my survival. This meant no extracurricular activities. This meant no socializing. This meant going from classes to the library to the dining hall and back to the dormitory, day in and day out.

Until my grades improved, I could not let myself enjoy the glamorous and glorified aspects of "college life." I had to confront some stark and bitter realities.

In college, whether you are at Harvard or you are at your local community college, no one is there to encourage you to study and to improve your situation. As a college student, you are on your own. You are constructing your own destiny.

102

My grades did improve by the end of my first semester. I finished by making the Dean's List, despite my poor first midterm grade. My professor for that class made a deal with me. If I demonstrated a dramatic improvement in my final exam, he would not consider my midterm grade when he calculated my final grade for the semester.

Despite making the Dean's List, I did have to spend a few subsequent semesters catching up on the academic and extracurricular dimensions of my college experience. I could not allow myself to get complacent just because I made the Dean's List. I had to rebuild the overall momentum that I had lost during the first semester. Academically, I wasted precious credits that I could have used to take much more interesting elective classes later in my college years. Thus, I needed to find classes that would satisfy multiple academic requirements so that I could afford to take electives as an upper classman.

Extracurricularly, I needed to join activities and work my way up the organizations and catch up with classmates who were a semester ahead of me in all respects.

So what did I learn from this experience?

I should have gone to Harvard with a specific post-Harvard goal in mind. In the same way that I entered Stuyvesant with the goal of getting into Harvard, I should have matriculated at Harvard with a focused objective.

Whether the goal was to get into a certain type of graduate school or to attain a certain type of job, having a solid goal would have guided me when I selected my courses. In addition, with focus, I would have been able to select extracurricular activities geared towards helping me achieve my post-Harvard goal. Having a post-Harvard goal would have enabled me to "hit the ground running" when I arrived at Harvard. With a goal, my first semester at Harvard would have been much more productive and enjoyable.

Paul J. Kim

2. What was your major at Harvard? Why did you select this major?

My major at Harvard was East Asian Studies.

Harvard does not call academic disciplines "majors" in the way that other colleges do. Harvard calls them "concentrations." However, for the remainder of this book, I will refer to my "concentration" as my "major." Harvard requires a student to declare a major at the end of the first year. This is a year earlier than at most other colleges. During the spring semester of my freshman year, I chose to pursue East Asian Studies. In all honesty, none of the other majors really appealed to me.

As you will recall, during my first semester, I took a course on Japanese history. This class held particular interest for me. The class was nicknamed "Shogun" and the subject matter it covered was the unification of Japan by three major warlords between 1560 and 1650. The set of events covered in this class coincided with James Clavell's novel, <u>Shogun</u>, which was made into a TV movie during the 1980s, starring Richard Chamberlain. I've always been a liberal artsy history buff and this class offered me my first opportunity to study something related to Asia in a formal academic setting.

Perhaps it was the opportunity to "find myself." I heard that people undergo numerous self-discovery episodes in college.

For me, I was thirsty for knowledge about my homeland and its history.

I was a Korean-American. Truthfully, though, I felt much more American than Korean. Yes, I spoke Korean at home, ate Korean food, attended a Korean church, had numerous Korean friends and visited Korea occasionally. However, inside, I felt a yearning to know about Korea and Asia on various dimensions. What was the region's history all about? I had also been hearing about the Asian economic miracle. What was that all about? What about the tumultuous relationship between Korea and Japan – how did it start and why did such animosity remain? What was the relationship between the United States and Asia really like? I heard about the Korean War and the Vietnam War. But were these two conflagrations the true extent of America's interaction with Asia? With Korea? I had developed a tremendous deal of curiosity about my ancestral homeland. Until I arrived at Harvard, I never had a formal academic opportunity to explore these types of issues.

At Harvard, I had the opportunity to study Korean history and Japanese sociology under the tutelage of tremendous academics who were at the forefront of Asia-related research. Here's an example. I studied about the industrialization of Asia as well as Japanese sociology under Professor Ezra Vogel. To give you an idea about how valued Professor Vogel's opinions were, let me share with you what I saw on television in the early 1990's. President George Bush (who was in office between 1989 - 1993) was on a trip to Japan. At a state dinner hosted by Prime Minister Miyazawa, President Bush collapsed due to fatigue and illness into the arms of Prime Minister Miyazawa. That same night, the ABC network's evening news show, "Nightline" (hosted by Ted Koppell), interviewed Professor Vogel live on national television to get his opinion on what happened in Japan and how it would impact US-Japan relations. That was when I realized how fortunate I was to study about Asian history at Harvard.

I was being educated by the premier Asian studies academics in the world.

Another example is my senior honors thesis advisor, Professor Carter Eckert. I wrote about the use of the national education system in Korea by President Park Chung Hee to help legitimize his regime (which came into being through a military coup). Professor Eckert was an expert on modern Korean history. His research took him to Korea on numerous occasions and even introduced him to President Park Chung Hee's family to get a first hand glimpse into the mind of the former President of Korea. He shared with me his learnings and views about Korea's modern history as he guided me on my thesis. This was definitely a privilege.

At the time I attended college, Asia's industrial prowess was on the rise and there was seemingly a premium placed on Asia-related knowledge. Prior to entering college, I gave brief thought to pursuing some type of an international career. Given my naïveté, I did not have any particulars in mind. However, it sounded "glamorous" and thus I rationalized my decision to myself.

I concluded that as an East Asian Studies major, I would ultimately pursue a career that spanned the Pacific.

With that in mind, I pursued a knowledge of Asian languages, namely, Korean and Japanese. I studied Korean for two years and Japanese for two years as well. In addition to the fact that language studies were a part of the academic requirement for my department, my rationale was that I would need to understand at least two Asian languages if I was going to have a successful pan-Pacific, international career.

3. *How did your course of study impact your Harvard experience?*

My Harvard experience would not have been the same without the East Asian Studies department. I learned a tremendous amount about Korea, Asia and Harvard as an institution. But most of all –

The experiences I underwent played an integral part in shaping my attitude about confronting challenges, meeting an important mentor and learning a critical skill.

Prior to arriving at Harvard, I was accustomed to a fairly lax studying regimen at Stuyvesant. As I shared earlier, I "optimized" on my time in order to maximize my studying productivity. This style of "understanding the main points and then moving on" worked well in high school. However, this type of approach did not work at Harvard. Intellectual rigor and thorough analysis were the standards. Intellectual rigor entailed reading volumes and volumes of books, considering various viewpoints on complex issues. Then, thorough analysis. This required writing extensively on your thoughts and reactions to what you just read.

I was not used to having to read three hundred or more pages per week per class. Imagine taking two or three classes, each with similar reading assignments, on top of language classes that meted out homework everyday!

On top of that, certain classes required concise, yet well-thought-out reaction papers before each class. Stress. Stress. Stress.

It was difficult to adjust. At its core, the three-year East Asian Studies experience was nothing short of an intellectual basic training/boot-camp. My instructors were the drill sergeants and I was a frail and frightened new recruit.

However, I did grow tremendously from the experience. The perseverance and tenacity that I developed while on the Stuyvesant Boys' Swim Team came in handy. I would say that this attitude grew stronger while in college. Despite the overwhelming academic environment that encapsulated me, I was not going to give up.

I was going to master the environment. The environment was not going to master me. I knew that I wasn't the brightest student at Harvard. But I also knew that I wasn't the dimmest. I was at Harvard because I belonged there.

115

With this in mind, I made up my mind firmly that I was going to graduate from Harvard with academic honors.

I thought of my parents and the hopes that they had for David and me when we came from Korea.

I thought of what my younger brother said to me in order to encourage me: "God brought us to this country and placed us respectively at Harvard and at West Point for a good reason. He was not going to abandon us in our time of struggle."

At the time, David was going through his own hardships as a new Cadet at West Point – severe physical, emotional and mental hardships called "hazing" inflicted by upperclassmen. Hearing such wisdom from David was one of the most poignant moments of my life. I realized how God was working through our family to encourage one another and to remain faithful to Him, especially during the difficult times.

***

By the time I was a senior at Harvard –

I developed a solid mentor relationship with a graduate student within the East Asian Studies department.

Hyung Gu was my instructor for a modern Korean history seminar which I took during my junior year. He taught me a strong lesson on being prepared. During one of our sessions, I was not prepared to address the analytical questions he posed during class. I got "raked over the coals" in front of my classmates. Hyung Gu is one of the proverbial "brightest bulbs on the chandelier." He is extremely intelligent and when he wants to make a point and make an example out of you, there is no escape. I was thoroughly embarrassed by him. But I was not angry with him. It was my fault for not being prepared. If I was prepared, then someone else would have been the target of the day. There was nothing personal in his criticism.

Afterwards, I learned of Hyung Gu's compassionate side. Upon concluding class, he asked me to accompany him to his office. He wanted to make sure that I was not too shaken by what happened. I respected him for caring enough to ask if I was okay. He didn't have to, but he did. After that experience, we began to develop a good friendship. I learned that Hyung Gu was a Korean who grew up in Japan and then in Canada. After completing college in Vancouver, Canada, Hyung Gu attended Harvard for his Ph.D.

A year after I graduated from Harvard, Hyung Gu also came to Korea. He was on a research visit for his doctorate dissertation. While in Korea, we spent time together as friends and even went out on double dates! Needless to say, our friendship grew very strong over time. We kept in touch when he left Korea for Japan and I returned to New York. Through email and phone calls, we stayed in contact. When I was re-adjusting to life in New York, after a three-year stay in Korea, Hyung Gu helped me tremendously by guiding me through some trying times. By the way –

Hyung Gu wrote a letter of recommendation for me when I applied to Columbia Business School. Remember, what I said about recommendation letters? It's easier to ask for a favor from a friend.

Hyung Gu attended my wedding in Seattle in 2002. Whenever he is in the New York City area, we dine together. Currently he is a professor at the University of British Columbia in Vancouver. He was and always will be my first mentor.

***

When I entered Harvard, I had trouble writing a five-page report. My Stuyvesant education did not prepare me on this front. By graduation, I had written countless multi-page reports, including an eighty five-page senior honors thesis. Needless to say –

My writing skills developed by quantum leaps and bounds. A solid writing ability comes in handy in a great variety of situations.

Whether it is for crafting short e-mails to friends or producing important documents on the job, writing skills are critical. My East Asian Studies experience truly helped with this area of my personal and professional development.

I've already mentioned the reaction papers that I wrote in response to books that I read for class. On top of that, final examinations were almost always in essay format. These final examinations lasted for approximately three hours each, during which, I had to develop my responses to essay questions in a persuasive and logical manner, based on the knowledge that I gained on the respective subject matter over the course of the semester. Fast forward ten years. At Johnson & Johnson, I work on strategic planning issues for the company's pharmaceutical business. I regularly produce multi-page written reports in a short time frame based on key strategic issues that I manage which affect the company's future. I unequivocally attribute this ability to the hardship and training I endured during my time as an East Asian Studies major.

In college, if my writing on an exam or a paper was not clear, concise and logically sound, I got a lower final grade for that class. In the grand scheme of things, it is not a big deal. Now at Johnson & Johnson, if my written reports and strategic recommendations are not clear, concise and logically sound, my managers will form a negative impression of my professional capabilities and my career will suffer. If my career suffers, then my finances will suffer. If my finances suffer, then my family will suffer. Indeed, writing is an integral skill.

Although it is not the only component of a person's career, writing ability definitely can make or break someone's professional outlook.

It is important to develop one's writing skills as thoroughly and as early as possible. This will lead to success in college and in the workplace.

4. Would you select this major again if you had the opportunity? Why? Why not?

Yes. However, I would also have minored in another subject area. East Asian Studies taught me a great deal about Asia and in particular, my homeland, Korea. In addition, it trained me in the fine art of writing. However, as I reflect back on my development, I realize that a greater part of my development was in the realm of knowledge; a smaller portion of my development entailed skill advancement.

Looking back at East Asian Studies as well as the numerous different majors that were offered to students at Harvard, I realize that each major offered students the opportunity to develop knowledge and skills. However, the ratio between knowledge cultivation and skill development differed by major.

Certain majors focused more heavily on knowledge, while others focused predominantly on skill development.

Before we continue, let me define the two terms "knowledge" and "skill." Knowledge is a collection of facts, ideas, and other content-oriented materials. In my view, majors that focus on knowledge are liberal arts areas such as History, Literature and Political Science. Skill is the ability to analyze or synthesize facts, ideas and other content-oriented materials for a specific purpose. Essentially, skill is the ability to do something productive with knowledge. Majors that focus on skills are the functional majors such as

Accounting, Finance, Engineering and Computer Science. Science majors such as Biology and Physics are somewhere in the middle between knowledge-oriented and skill-oriented.

After commencement, most graduates are set either to start working in the "real world" or to continue their education in graduate school. My recommendation is the following.

If a person's goal is to start working immediately after college, she should major in an area that focuses on skill development.

This will make the person attractive to potential employers because by the time the person joins the company, she will have abilities that are readily applicable in the company's day-to-day business dealings. Although some employers tout their "training programs" and "development plans for new employees," they are business people and are focused on maximizing their profits. It is expensive to train a new employee. The more that a new employee needs to learn about how to contribute to the business, the more expensive it is to train that person. Therefore, employers will generally prefer new employees who already have a foundation of skills. In other words, if a person is interested in joining the finance sector, then she should have a solid grasp of accounting and/or finance. If a person is interested in joining the technology sector, then she should have a solid understanding of critical topics such as engineering and/or computer science. These are not hard and fast rules, but prevalently applicable enough in the "real world."

Regarding training programs, employers usually select liberal arts graduates only if they exhibit great potential to pick up business skills fast enough so that within a short period of time, they can contribute as well as those who have undergraduate business training. With this in mind –

126

Employers are more likely to hire liberal arts majors from competitive colleges than from non-competitive colleges.

I was one of these liberal arts majors from a top-caliber school who was selected by a management consulting company. I will discuss this in greater detail later on in the book.

If a person is focused on graduate school, then she should generally pursue a knowledge-oriented major.

By graduate school, I do not mean law school (JD degree), business school (MBA degree) or medical school (MD degree). These three are considered professional programs. Anyone who graduates with a four-year college degree and takes the LSAT exam is eligible to apply to, and if admitted, attend law school. Anyone who graduates with a four-year college degree and takes the GMAT exam is eligible to apply to, and if admitted, attend business school. Anyone who graduates with a four-year college degree, takes the MCAT exam and fulfills the "pre-medical" college course requirements is eligible to apply to, and if admitted, attend medical school. For each of these three professional programs, there are no requirements regarding the major that the student must pursue. Upon completion, the person is awarded a JD, a MBA or a MD degree. These are considered "professional programs" because they prepare a person for a particular type of professional career.

However, if a person would like to attend graduate school for a master's degree or even a doctorate degree in a certain academic area, that person must select that academic area (or a similar one) as his or her undergraduate major. For example, if a person plans to pursue a Ph.D. in English Literature so that she can pursue a professorship, she should major in English Literature in college. Graduate schools award "advanced" degrees. I believe that this term is a shorter version of the term "advanced knowledge" degree. By furthering one's education in the academic subject, a person is furthering her knowledge that she can share with others.

If a person is not certain if she will pursue a job, a professional program or graduate school, just as I was when I first entered college, then I believe the best course of action is to major in a knowledge-oriented area and minor in a skill-oriented area.

This arrangement will enable the person to retain as many options as possible. Anything can happen in college and a person's future plans can change dramatically. As for me –

Majoring in East Asian Studies was a great opportunity. However, I should have minored in a business-related area.

Harvard had an exchange program with the Massachusetts Institute of Technology. I should have taken some accounting, finance and marketing classes at MIT's undergraduate business program. That way, I would have been optimally prepared for my future "international" career dealing with Asia. Flexibility is critical to future planning. Flexibility should be a factor when a person selects her course of study in college.

5. *What career did you want to pursue with your major?*

At Harvard, as well as at many other competitive colleges, a large number of students pursue one of the following five post-college endeavors, also known as "exit strategies." The first one is graduate school in pursuit of a master's degree or a doctorate degree in a certain academic area. The second is medical school. The third is law school. The fourth is management consulting. The fifth is investment banking/finance. At many competitive schools, these five alternatives, fine as they may be, garner much more than their fair share of attention. There are a plethora of fine post-college pursuits outside of these five, but they are not as conspicuous as these five. Hence, many students do not feel empowered to pursue something outside of these five. With that in mind, students bow to peer pressure and/or parental suggestions.

I was one of these students who selected from among these five options. As mentioned above, I desired an international dimension to my career. Upon review –

I decided law school would be my pursuit. I would practice law on the international level.

Truth be told, I was not totally convinced this was right for me. I selected this due to a combination of a process of elimination and outside influence. I eliminated grad school because I saw too many Ph.D.'s struggling financially. I eliminated medical school because I am not comfortable with physiology (i.e., other people's blood) and I had heard about the awful struggle it took to become a doctor – four years of college, four years of medical school and anywhere between three to six years of residency in which a person works extremely long hours for minimal pay, only to become an attending physician in an era where managed care organizations and malpractice lawsuits hindered physicians from fully realizing their professional and financial potential. I eliminated management consulting and investment banking/finance because I never had a passion for business while in college. I also felt that my major was not conducive to pursuing these two "exit strategies."

With those four choices out of the way, I chose law school. East Asian Studies prepared me to read great amounts and write on what I read. Law school seemed to require the same types of skills. Furthermore, everyone was doing it. It seemed as though every other person with whom I spoke indicated that she was headed to law school. I rationalized my decision by telling myself, "Harvard kids are smart. If they are focused on law school, they must know something I don't. Let's see where this goes." It was a classic lemming mentality situation. Unfortunately, I found out, I was among many who selected law school for the same process of elimination logic.

Essentially, law school was a choice for those who did not know what they truly wanted to pursue after college.

The law seemed to offer security and prestige. For a person without any solid direction, it was a good fallback alternative.

6. What is management consulting? What is investment banking? How do college graduates benefit by going into these fields?

Management consulting and investment banking/finance are fine post-college pursuits. These two industries provide critical business services to corporate clients worldwide.

Businesses throughout the world grapple with the following equation:

Revenues – Expenditures = Profits

135

Revenues are monies collected from customers for products and/or services sold to them. Expenditures are the monies spent by the provider of the products and/or services in the process of producing and selling her wares. Profits are monies that are left over after expenditures have been spent.

Management consultants work with clients to help them maximize their revenues and/or to minimize their expenditures, thereby maximizing the client's profits.

Investment bankers work with clients to access the monetary resources required to implement the strategies and tactics designed to maximize revenues and/or minimize expenditures.

The following is a very basic illustration of what management consulting firms and investment banks do.

A company that makes and sells televisions in the United States wants to improve its profitability. It hires a management consulting firm that recommends that the company consider selling its televisions also in Canada. This will improve the company's total revenues. But in addition, the management consulting firm recommends that the client company build a television factory in Canada. This will minimize expenditures related to delivering televisions for sale in Canada as well as tariffs (taxes imposed by the government of the importing country) that the company may face when exporting televisions into Canada. By following this strategy of international expansion, the client should maximize its profits.

But how will the company get the money to build the new factory in Canada? It does not have any money in the bank. Therefore, the company hires an investment bank to raise the money required to build the factory. The investment bank seeks out potential investors who are willing and able to lend the

137

company the large amount of money it needs to expand into Canada. Over time, the company follows the strategy set by the management consulting firm with the money acquired for it by the investment bank. Ultimately, this will increase the company's profits.

***

Joining a management consulting firm or an investment bank could be a fantastic learning and development opportunity for a college graduate. Management consulting firms and investment banks are constantly solving business problems such as the illustration above. By constant engagement in such endeavors –

College graduates learn very quickly about the business world and the principles that drive business success and failure.

In addition, these firms are great at teaching young college graduates very important skills. These include strategic and analytical capabilities such as analyzing the competitive and regulatory environment of a potential new market and identifying and evaluating different capitalization options for clients. Moreover, there are day-to-day skills development such as working with Excel spreadsheets, creating PowerPoint presentations and analyzing financial statements.

These firms actively recruit candidates from among college students who demonstrate potential to grow and contribute meaningfully to their endeavors. They find these students among those who studied business related topics in college, had solid business experience prior to graduation and/or studied liberal arts but demonstrate a particular potential for success.

Management consulting firms and investment banks are structured with four main levels of professionals, depending on their capability levels.

At Bain & Company, my former management consulting company, the four levels were: Partner/Vice President, Manager, Consultant and Associate Consultant. At JP Morgan (now called "JP Morgan Chase" due to a recent merger with Chase Manhattan Bank), my former investment bank/financial services firm, the four levels were: Managing Director, Vice President, Associate and Analyst. The four respective levels in each company are analogous to one another in their specific order of listing.

College students are recruited into Associate Consultant positions at Bain and Analyst positions at JP Morgan.

I will use a management consulting firm's structure to provide a simple illustration of how these four levels interact. A management consulting firm is like a restaurant. A Partner is like the owner of a restaurant. She has to constantly seek out customers and persuade them to eat at the restaurant. Once a customer comes into the restaurant, she is seated at a table and a waitress comes by and becomes the customer's main server.

A Manager is like the waitress because she manages all aspects of the client engagement. Most importantly, the waitress works with the customer to identify what the customer needs or makes suggestions on what the customer may want to eat. Then the waitress takes the customer's order and brings it to the kitchen where the chef prepares the meal.

A Consultant (usually a recruit from a top-tier MBA program) is like the chef. She prepares the meal according to the customer's order and the waitress' particular instructions on how to prepare the order (i.e., "a steak, medium-rare"). In order to prepare the meal, however, the chef needs to have proper ingredients and cookware. So, she tells the kitchen assistant to take care of many menial tasks that help to facilitate the chef's cooking efforts.

An Associate Consultant is like the kitchen assistant. The kitchen assistant does everything that the chef asks her to do, including washing dishes, cleaning tables, shopping for ingredients and preparing certain ingredients in advance. If the kitchen assistant is very talented, she may be allowed to prepare side dishes, such as soups and salads, but never the main meal.

After the meal is prepared, the waitress brings it to the customer. The owner follows up by making sure everything is fine. Ultimately, the customer consumes the meal and pays the owner before leaving. If the customer is satisfied, she returns and/or recommends the restaurant to others.

7. What extracurricular activities or part-time jobs do you recommend in college?

In line with my earlier suggestion that a person should have a post-college goal upon matriculation, my suggestion is to –

Engage in extracurricular activities and/or part-time jobs that are connected directly to one's post-college goal.

Of course, selecting certain extracurricular activities and/or part-time jobs depends on one's personal interests as well as financial realities.

143

My main extracurricular activities and part-time jobs were the following –

I worked as a law clerk at a local Boston law firm, served as a student officer in a large off-campus church group and sang with a semi-professional student a cappella group.

I clerked at Samek & Faneuil, a local Boston law firm, for three years. It was a small firm, with only two attorneys, focusing on civil cases (i.e., non-criminal). During my sophomore year, having decided that I was going to attend law school, I thought that it would help my chances if I worked in a law firm and learned about the legal world.

In all honesty, I was a naïve young man who was desperate to find a meaningful activity outside of class, one that I could put on my resume. I visited Harvard's career service office for part-time job listings. I could not find any listings that appealed to me or for which I felt qualified. Hence, I took matters into my own hands.

I found Samek & Faneuil through the local yellow pages.

I literally went through the Boston yellow pages, identified law firms that focused on corporate law, prepared and sent out cover letters and resumes. Mr. Samek called me in for an interview. I must have made a positive impression on him during our conversation because he offered me a job at the end of the interview. I recall him stating that he liked my initiative.

My job at Samek & Faneuil was not very value-added, in retrospect. My role was that of a glorified errand boy. I filed documents for the attorneys at the Suffolk County Courthouse, the same one portrayed on the ABC television show, "The Practice." In addition, I maintained certain client files, updating them with pertinent information. But given my lack of

145

experience, I'm grateful for the chance to work at his firm. Mr. Samek was my first employer. He gave me my first professional opportunity.

***

In addition to clerking at Samek & Faneuil, I served as a student officer of a local church college group. It was a Korean-American church located in suburban Boston. I decided to attend that church upon the suggestion of Reverend Chang of my home church in Flushing. The Korean Presbyterian Church in Boston was its name. It no longer exists, though, because the congregation split up about a year or two after my college graduation.

The college group had students from a large collection of local colleges including Harvard, Boston University, Wellesley College, MIT, Boston College, Tufts University and Gordon College. The group was fairly large, about one hundred or so students. The college group selected its officers every year. During my junior year, I was selected as an officer.

I decided to accept my college group officer position because I realized the importance of having organizational experience for the future.

I forecasted that I would likely be working in large organizations of people after college. Hence, this position offered an opportunity to learn about working in an organizational setting on a small scale.

This position was my first real "leadership" position in a working organization. It taught me a number of good lessons. The most important was that not everyone can be a leader, but anyone can be a manager. A manager is a person who is responsible to implement ideas and goals that are important to an organization. A leader is a person who comes up with the ideas and encourages those around him/her to set goals for the organization. I discovered that each of the officers, including the President, was a manager. The college group pastor was our leader. I do not recall the officer group having meaningful input into setting visions for the college group nor establishing goals. The college group needed work horses to get administrative things done. The officers served this purpose as managers. None of us was a leader.

***

College activities were not all work. There was also some fun involved.

During the second half of my freshman year, I joined the Callbacks, a semi-professional singing group.

I had to audition for the group and compete with several other students who were interested in singing. My only singing experience prior to college was singing in my church choir in elementary school.

Furthermore, I could not (and still cannot) read sheet music. Nevertheless, I developed a passion for singing and music. I taught myself to play the guitar while in junior high school, so why couldn't I teach myself to sing in a musical group?

The Callbacks was a co-ed (men and women together) *a cappella* group of twelve to fifteen members covering all four singing parts – soprano, alto, tenor and bass. There was a range of members because each year, we had members graduating as well as new members joining. I sang as a tenor. *A cappella* is singing without musical accompaniment. Essentially, one member sings the solo while the other members replicate with their voices the music that would be played by instruments. If you've never heard collegiate *a cappella*, you are missing a fantastic musical experience!

The Callbacks were a fun bunch of friends. At Harvard, there were no university-sanctioned fraternities or sororities. Hence, membership in an *a cappella* group was a substitute. I made lasting friendships in the Callbacks. We recently had a reunion in upstate New York for Callbacks who sang during the early 1990s. My wife Yuni and I reconnected with other members and their spouses. Furthermore, when I proposed to my wife Yuni, I planned the proposal secretly with the current generation of Callbacks. I brought Yuni up to Harvard and to my old dormitory, Adams House. I arranged for the Callbacks to await us at a student lounge area and serenade Yuni when we arrived. They sang a couple of great romantic tunes. Afterwards, I proposed to Yuni. It was one of the most memorable moments of our lives.

The Callbacks have great affinity for one another. Once a Callback, always a Callback.

Extracurricular activities and/or part-time jobs are an integral part of a person's college experience.

It is critical that a person select activities or jobs that are in line with one's future goals, can teach a person valuable skills and provide opportunities to establish important, long-lasting relationships.

There is no one activity or job that college students should all experience. The selections are unique to each student, but the selections should be made along the three criteria mentioned above.

Paul J. Kim

8. How should a student spend the summers? How did you spend your summers?

There are two productive ways to spend one's summers.

The first way is to find a summer job that is connected to one's post-college goals.

For example, if a student is interested in becoming an investment banker, then she might want find a summer job with an investment bank or the finance department of a company. If a student is interested in joining a publishing company, she might want to find a summer position with a publishing company. The point is that there are many different summer internships for college students in a variety of professional areas. It is up to the student to determine which professional area is of interest to her and to pursue a position aggressively creatively.

The second way is to take classes in one's academic major and gain college credits toward graduation.

Summer classes tend to be graded less stringently. Hence, if there is a mandatory class that a student dreads, then the summer might be a good time to take it. For example, Organic Chemistry is a difficult class, but it is a requirement for pre-medical students at all colleges. I know of a number of friends who decided to stay at Harvard over a summer and take that class. Not only was the grading a bit less stringent than during the regular academic year, my friends were able to focus all of their attention on Organic Chemistry because it was the only class that they took over the summer. It is not surprising that many of them were happy with their grades at the end of the summer.

***

I spent my summers in the following way. As mentioned above, I did not have the most productive freshman year. Not only did I suffer setbacks with academics and extracurriculars, I also missed opportunities to search for summer endeavors. Hence, I decided to reach out and network with personal contacts in New York to see if any opportunities existed.

The summer after my freshman year, I returned to New York and worked as a teaching assistant at CCB English School.

This is where I had studied for the Stuyvesant High School entrance examination and the SAT. It was a good experience for me in that it introduced me to a number of simple principles related to work. One, develop discipline in terms of daily work schedule. Basically, I learned to get to work earlier than I was expected to. This allowed me to get all of my work done and find new opportunities for growth. Two, respect your teammates. Every person contributes something to the team. For that, each person should be respected. Three, loyalty is to be commended. Mr. Sohn, the founder and proprietor of CCB English School provided David and me with the training necessary to gain admission to Stuyvesant High School that led to countless opportunities for both of us. I felt a great deal of loyalty to him and still do. He gave me an opportunity to spend the summer with him and to learn his business.

***

During the summer after my sophomore year, I killed two birds with one stone. I secured a summer job at a large Korean law firm and I gained college credits by studying abroad at a Korean university.

First, the Korean law firm experience. A family friend in Korea knew the managing partner of a growing Korean law firm. With that connection, I found myself working at his law firm as an English editor and translator. As I alluded to above, I considered going to law school after graduating from college. With that in mind, I thought that having some experience working at a large law firm would be helpful for my future legal career. I had been working as a clerk at a local Boston firm, Samek & Faneuil. I felt that I needed exposure to the law at a larger firm and on a more international level.

Second, the Korean university experience. I enrolled at the International Division of Yonsei University. At Yonsei, I took two classes: Korean International Relations and Korean Politics. These classes provided me with enough academic credits to lighten my graduation requirements by two classes at Harvard. In addition, my coursework helped to prepare me for a number of challenging classes at Harvard within the East Asian Studies department.

***

During the summer after my junior year Harvard, I spent the summer in Hakodate, Hokkaido, Japan. I wanted to experience living in Japan, given that I had studied Japanese and Japanese sociology at Harvard.

With that, I enrolled in a home-stay language program. I lived with a Japanese family for twelve weeks and attended a daily language school. The Yoshida family was a wonderful family. I am grateful to them for their generosity in opening up their home to me. They provided me with my own room, fed me daily and went out of their way to help me learn about the Japanese language and culture. I became another son to them. This concept at first was a bit odd. Let me explain. I was twenty-two years old when I arrived in Japan. Mr. Yoshida was in his early forties. Mrs. Yoshida was in her early thirties. Their children were in kindergarten and elementary school. I was of the age to have passed for Mrs. Yoshida's younger brother, not her home-stay son. Nevertheless, I took to my role very smoothly. By the end of the summer, my Japanese improved dramatically. Upon returning to Harvard, I took a Japanese language proficiency exam, the results of which allowed me to skip an entire level of Japanese language studies, from beginner directly to advanced. It was a productive summer indeed.

9. If you could have done two things differently while in college, what would they be?

First, I should have participated in the debate team and practiced my debating skills.

In the professional world, a person's writing ability is extremely important. However, a person's speaking ability is even more critical.

By speaking ability, I mean the ability to analyze another person's statements during a conversation and deliver immediate comments that logically address the other person's statements and convey one's own thoughts in a clear, concise and deliberate manner. Fundamentally, this is the skill that is developed by those on a debate team. More importantly, this is the skill that is most readily perceived by a person's colleagues in a corporate setting, or in any setting for that matter. Every interaction entails speaking to others. Whether in a large conference room, in a hallway during breaks or even in a restroom, people form perceptions about a person by the way that she speaks. It is extremely important to develop this ability. Perhaps I should have joined the debate team at the high school level and stayed with it throughout college?

Second, I should have continued to study Spanish throughout college.

I began learning Spanish in seventh grade and studied it until I completed my first year of college. Today, after seven years of Spanish, I can barely order food at a Spanish restaurant. I am a bit embarrassed to admit it. Spanish is a fantastic language to know. It is an important language in America and it will become an even more important language in the future, given the growing Hispanic population. I should have continued to study it so that I could have opened up a whole new world of opportunity for myself.

Paul J. Kim

IV. My Career Development

1. What are your career highlights to date? What are the key lessons that you learned along the way? How did you guide your career? Did anyone help you along the way?

Since my college days, I have held a variety of different jobs. I acquired each of these jobs in unique ways. In addition, I have also learned a number of very important lessons about the working world and how a person should develop a career. The following chapters are arranged in chronological order and will illustrate the manner in which I developed my own career.

2. *Samek & Faneuil – Law Clerk*

Previously, I shared that I acquired my job as a law clerk at Samek & Faneuil by looking up law firms in Boston and mailing my resume to them. I succeeded in securing this job after meeting with Mr. Samek. While I worked at his firm until college graduation, I learned the following key lesson –

Creativity can help find a golden opportunity.

During my sophomore year, I was hungry and desperate for a solid extracurricular activity that involved the law. I visited the Harvard career service office to look for any opportunities. I found only leftovers – basically, those opportunities that no one else wanted. I was disappointed, but I was not going to give up. I felt as though I did not exhaust all of my options. If Harvard will not provide options for me, then I will create my own options. Where else could I find a list of law firms that might be looking for a part-time student to work for them? The phone book, of course!!! I found a local phone book and sent out about twenty-five or so cover letters and resumes inquiring if the law firms had an opportunity for an aspiring future lawyer. Mr. Samek was the only one who asked me to come in for an interview. I jumped at the chance and showed up for my meeting. The rest was history. Mr. Samek gave me my first professional job. I parlayed this opportunity into greater and greater opportunities in my future career.

3. *CJ International – Law Clerk*

During the summer between my sophomore and junior year at Harvard, I worked as a law clerk at a growing Korean law firm, CJ International. Given that I wanted to enter into the field of international law, I sought out an opportunity to work at a law firm that practiced law at a global level. CJ International had a number of clients dealing with cross-border issues. The clients included Korean firms dealing with overseas business partners as well as non-Korean firms (mostly American, British and Japanese) doing business in Korea. My role was to edit English

171

documents as well as to translate some Korean documents into English. I was not a lawyer, so I did not fully understand the content of the documents I managed. Clearly, I had to work with attorneys who could clarify matters for me.

The manner in which I secured my opportunity at CJ International taught me a key lesson –

Personal connections have the most positive impact on a person's job search.

I found the CJ International job because my father's closest mentor in Korea knew the managing partner of the firm. Mr. Chi attended church with Dr. Kim, the head of CJ International. Prior to my father calling Mr. Chi and asking if he knew of any contacts at law firms, I thought that my goal of working at an international law firm during the summer would not be realized. Hence, I applied to and was accepted to Yonsei University's International Division to take classes in Korea and get college credit for my East Asian Studies graduation requirements. I thought that this would be my only summer activity.

I was pleasantly corrected. Mr. Chi called back and told me of the CJ International opportunity. I was ecstatic! Not only would I get college credit towards my major over the summer, I would get work experience in my future career area! By the way, Samek & Faneuil factored into this CJ International opportunity because Dr. Kim saw my resume and saw that I had real-life experience working at a law firm in Boston. Thank you Mr. Samek. Thank you Mr. Chi. Thank you Dr. Kim. By the way, a Harvard classmate also worked at CJ International that summer as a law clerk. She got her job because her father knew Dr. Kim as well.

Paul J. Kim

4. *Lee & Ko – Researcher/Translator*

My next job was as a researcher/translator at Lee & Ko, at the time, Korea's second largest law firm (as measured by number of attorneys). As a senior, at Harvard, I wanted to graduate and go out to Korea to couple my academic understanding of my homeland with real-life experiences. In light of my legal interests, I decided to look for an opportunity in Korea to work as a full-time law clerk at a large Korean law firm that practiced international law. I went to the library at Harvard Law School and looked up the names and addresses of Korea's largest law firms in the Martindale-Hubbell directory. I sent out cover letters and resumes to these firms. Soon thereafter, I got a call from Lee & Ko. Mr. Lee was going to be on a business trip to New York City. He wanted to meet me in Manhattan for a lunch interview. Lee & Ko offered to fly me to New York. How could I resist? What Mr. Lee said to me during the interview taught me my first two lessons –

A degree from a prestigious school does indeed open doors.

Businesses like to hire those who have worked for the competition.

Mr. Lee shared with me that he attended Seoul National University for his law degree. Then, he attended Harvard Law School where he received two additional law degrees. The primary reason that he wanted to meet me was that I attended Harvard, just as he did. He had faith in Harvard students because of the reputation of the school. Then he told me why he was going to make me an offer to join his firm in Korea. I had worked at CJ International, one of his competitor law firms in Korea. He reasoned that if CJ International believed in my abilities enough to employ me for a summer, then he had further faith that I could do the job required at his firm. At the end of lunch, Mr. Lee wrote me a personal check for my travel expenses to New York City from Boston. Furthermore, he told me that his secretary would send an official "offer letter" and a round-trip airline ticket between New York City and Seoul.

Soon after graduation, I flew to Korea and began my job at Lee & Ko. I thought my job was going to teach me substantive things about international law, but it did not. My role entailed translating Mr. Lee's personal correspondences into English. Only on infrequent occasions, I was able to work on legal documents. Within a short time, I grew uncomfortable with my position at Lee & Ko. This taught me my third lesson –

Find a job that will teach you marketable skills for the future.

I was not learning anything concrete about international law. For example, issues such as how international disputes occurred, who the arguing parties were, how resolution is brought about, etc. Given that I was not yet a lawyer, I knew that my role would remain limited. Hence, I began to talk with foreign lawyers (those who received their attorney licenses outside of Korea, predominantly in America) at the firm about my situation.

My discussions with them taught me my fourth lesson –

Seek advice from people you trust because you will probably get some good advice.

178

I engaged these lawyers for advice about what I can do to improve my job at Lee & Ko. They gave me more than I expected. They questioned why I wanted to become a lawyer. They were very frank with me in sharing how they hated being lawyers. No other profession had so many unhappy members. Why would I want to join such a profession? At first, I was concerned that they were misguiding me. But all of them professed the same dislike for the law. In addition, I recalled that I selected the law not because I had a passion for it but because I felt as though I had no other choice. In the end, I realized that they were being honest with me and were giving me reliable advice.

After much contemplation, I decided that I was not going to be a lawyer. But there was a problem. I was in Korea with Lee & Ko. If I left Lee & Ko, then I would have to leave Korea. I had been in Korea only for a few months. I was not ready to return to America.

What would I do? I decided to apply my fourth lesson from Lee & Ko. I spoke with a friend named Joanne whom I had met in Korean-American social groups. She was an older-sister figure who was a Dartmouth graduate and a former management consultant with Bain & Company at its Boston headquarters. She told me about how management consulting firms such as Bain and its rivals such as McKinsey and the Boston Consulting Group regularly hired students from prestigious liberal arts colleges and trained them in business strategies and analysis. She suggested that I apply to the Seoul offices of these firms, particularly given that these Seoul offices were looking to hire American-educated, English-speaking employees.

5. *Bain & Company – Associate Consultant*

I applied to the Seoul offices of a number of different management consulting companies. I decided to join Bain & Company as an Associate Consultant. When I first came out to Korea, my intent was to stay for only a year and return to America and attend law school to become a lawyer. Now, my goal was to learn as much as I could about the business world and about Asia. Bain would provide me with this opportunity. During my tenure at Bain, I traveled throughout Asia including Tokyo, Hong Kong,

Singapore and Thailand. My assignments even entailed working with colleagues from Australia. I was involved in a substantive way on many projects. For example, I was solely responsible for the Korean portion of an American automobile product company's pan-Asian market-entry strategy project. In addition, I coordinated the benchmarking research efforts of consultants from five different countries for a Korean telecommunications industry client. Indeed, this was the international career that I had envisioned for myself while in college. It was a great opportunity. To this day, I count my Bain experience as one of my most important career experiences.

During my tenure at Bain, I learned a number of key career-related lessons. My first lesson –

Start your career in a country where you are completely comfortable with the language.

Yes, Korea is my homeland. Yes, I spoke Korean at home. Yes, I studied Korean in college. However, I was not fluent in Korean, particularly business Korean. Becoming familiar with business Korean was a challenge in addition to the primary challenge of learning about business strategies and analytics. Usually, liberal arts graduates joining management consulting firms only have to endeavor to learn business fundamentals. I had to learn a new language on top of that. This placed an immense amount of pressure on me during my first year at Bain. This was pressure that my Korean-educated counterparts did not encounter. Hence, I quickly felt that I was falling behind my counterparts in terms of professional development. To overcome this obstacle, I met with a language tutor regularly before work and became fluent in a year. During my second year, my business Korean became fluent enough so that I could manage international projects independently.

My second lesson –

Having a great boss is better than having a great job.

My job at Bain was fantastic. My comments above will attest to that. However, during my first year, I seriously contemplated quitting and returning to America. At the time, I was on an extended project and working with two senior consultants. I did not have a good relationship with them. In fairness, I must take some responsibility for the situation. I was not as productive as I could have been on the team because of my language issue as well as a bout of homesickness.

However, my case team leaders did not improve the situation. Rather than engaging me to understand the root of the problem and to resolve it together, they subjected me to derogatory and condescending comments almost on a daily basis. It was absolutely degrading. I had never in my life been treated so badly by anyone. Normally, I would have spoken up to explain the situation. However, given their treatment, I decided that I could not trust them with anything, especially my personal thoughts. I decided to suffer through the case assignment. After finishing the assignment, I resolved never to work with these individuals again, if I could. Furthermore, I planned to quit Bain upon reaching my one-year anniversary.

The main reason why I did not leave Bain at the end of my first year was because I found two mentors who helped me to put my situation into perspective. This resolution resulted in my third key lesson –

Find a good mentor or an ally at your job.

Tommy and Sam were both Consultants who joined Bain roughly at the same time that I did. They had recently graduated from Columbia Business School and Harvard Business School, respectively. Coincidentally, Tommy grew up in Flushing and attended Brooklyn Tech and then Columbia

University. Sam grew up in California and attended MIT. We had many commonalities. But most importantly, we were all Korean-Americans living and working in Seoul, undergoing similar challenges. We formed a close friendship during our first year at Bain.

Tommy had been observing my case assignment situation and sensed that I was miserable. During an office outing, Tommy invited me to a one-on-one conversation. He wanted to know how I was doing. But more importantly, he wanted to help me see the bigger picture. Basically, he told me that there are two main reasons for a person leaving a job. Either the person is running away from something he dislikes or the person is running towards something that he prefers. His opinion was that I was running away from a situation that I did not like. He then challenged me to consider the following questions.

Did I make a good-faith effort to confront the issues that bothered me? Was my case assignment a permanent one or a temporary one that was scheduled to end within a reasonable period of time? What would I do upon returning to America? If I ran away from this situation, would I be able to stand and fight the next time something similar happened?

I did not quit when I was at Harvard. I was not going to quit at Bain.

Tommy also provided pivotal advice about crafting my future career direction. He impressed upon me the importance of getting my MBA, a Master of Business Administration degree. I was a liberal arts major in the business world. My long-term career development, whether in consulting or in any other industry, required that I understand the fundamentals of business, including accounting, finance, marketing and statistics. Given that I did not study these topics in college, I needed to return to school and learn these critical skills as soon as possible. Learning the basics in a formal academic setting would be much more beneficial than trying to teach these skills to myself on the job because my errors while learning on the job could cause unnecessary damage to my career. Based on his urging, I decided to prepare myself for my graduate business education.

In 1997, I resigned from Bain & Company and returned to New York City after three years in Korea. The specific impetus of my return was Mom's health. She had been ill since 1996 and her condition seemed to worsen. I decided to forego a third-year assignment with Bain at the firm's Toronto office and quickly return to America. This was a pivotal moment in my career development. I forged my philosophical outlook regarding my professional career. This formed the fourth and most important lesson from Bain –

Family is more important than career opportunities.

Until the spring of 1997, my plan was to transition to the Toronto office and continue with my consulting in Canada until I applied to business schools. However, with Mom's ailment, I decided to stop my career at Bain on very short notice. When I returned to America, I did not have any jobs lined up nor did I have any graduate school acceptances. Within a period of a month, I went from jet setting throughout Asia on international consulting assignments to being unemployed in New York City and living with my parents.

This was not the time to think of myself. I needed to think about my parents and their situation. Mom was critically ill from a hematological condition (a blood-related illness) and needed someone to be with her while Dad worked during the day. Dad's medical insurance covered Mom's treatment costs, hence, it was important that he performed well at his job. Having me at home would provide him with a degree of ease about Mom during the day. While Dad was at work, I stayed at home with Mom, accompanying her regularly to the hospital, picking up medications for her at the local pharmacy and managing insurance paperwork.

I stayed at home with Mom for about nine months.

6. JP Morgan – Financial Analyst

In early 1998, Mom began to recover slowly. With this encouraging news, I decided that I needed to re-enter the working world. During the winter of 1997, I applied to business schools and was awaiting their replies. Until I matriculated at business school in the fall, I needed to work and earn some money. I spoke with some short-term employment agencies specializing in the finance industry. Based upon my lack of accounting and finance skills, I wanted to learn as much as I could about this area on-the-job before entering school. Also, since I planned to start school in

191

half a year, it would have been improper to secure a "full-time" job and then leave only after six months.

Within a short time, I found an opportunity to work for JP Morgan. I made sure that my soon-to-be boss knew that I was leaving by August of 1998 and that he was amenable to this arrangement.

I began work as a Financial Analyst in the corporate technology financial control area. This department handled budgets dealing with information technology equipment used throughout a certain division of JP Morgan. I acquired important skills dealing with excel spreadsheets and budgets during my six months. But more importantly, I learned a key lesson –

A person's skills are more important than a person's prestigious background.

Of course, if you have skills and a prestigious background, then you are in a golden situation.

When I entered JP Morgan, I naïvely thought that my colleagues would mostly be graduates of Ivy League colleges and other competitive schools. JP Morgan was a prestigious Wall Street firm. Of course it would focus on populating its ranks with graduates of schools with commensurate status, I thought to myself.

This was not the case at all! In my department of fifteen individuals, I was the only one with an Ivy League degree. Everyone else graduated from schools that I did not even consider attending because I was so fixated on going to an Ivy League university. These schools included Baruch College, Hunter College and Scranton University. These are fine schools in their own right. However, they are not generally considered "prestigious" in the same manner as Ivy League universities.

I also noticed another trend. I was the only one without an undergraduate business degree. My colleagues did not have prestigious educational backgrounds, but developed marketable skills while in college. Now, they were impact players within JP Morgan. I was a liberal arts college graduate who demonstrated the potential to develop quickly and catch up. This was my boss' evaluation of my candidacy. This was in line with the perspective that my former management consulting firm had about my prestigious liberal arts college background when it decided to hire me.

Within six months, I learned necessary skills and caught up with my colleagues. But during my six months, I also noticed that the only other liberal arts majors who worked at JP Morgan were those from Ivy League schools. Colleagues from less-competitive colleges were almost always former business majors. Then it dawned upon me that in the working world, people with marketable backgrounds (in other words, business education and work experience) are in greater demand than people with just prestigious backgrounds (in other words, Ivy League-caliber

194

liberal arts backgrounds). With this in mind, I was all-the-more resolved to attend business school and develop my understanding of fundamental business skills.

Paul J. Kim

7. Columbia Business School – MBA Student

In August 1998, I matriculated at Columbia Business School. Columbia offered me an opportunity to couple a prestigious background with a solid marketable background. I took a wide variety of courses that built my business acumen, including accounting, finance, marketing, statistics, operations management, strategy and organizational management. I enjoyed the academic aspects of business school very much. However, I quickly learned that academics, while extremely important, needed to take a back seat to my career development.

As a student at Columbia Business School, I guided my activities by two important lessons. My first lesson–

Success in a MBA program is not measured by a person's grades, but whether or not she secures a good job.

My finance professor taught me the concept of Return on Investment. I applied it to my Columbia experience. "ROI," as it is commonly called, is an assessment of the gains garnered as a result of the resources and efforts expended for an endeavor. Attending Columbia Business School entailed roughly $70,000 and a great deal of personal time.

What ROI did I truly need for my time, money and efforts while at Columbia Business School? Good grades? Yes, but I needed something more important than that. I needed a good paying and worthwhile job.

How else would I pay off my newly incurred $70,000 debt? Obviously, my MBA education alone will not enable me to pay my bills. A solid job will.

What made my situational analysis even better was that I discovered that many employers who recruited from Columbia did not ask about a candidate's grades! This meant that as long as I passed my classes, my future employer would most likely not care what grades I achieved. Therefore, my primary concern was to secure a job that would satisfy me personally and financially in the long run. With this in mind, my job search for a summer internship and then a full-time job took precedence over my grades. Of course, I didn't flounder in class. I made the Dean's List and in my final semester at Columbia, I received all A's.

The second important lesson was that –

The highest-paying jobs are not always the best.

Columbia Business School is traditionally a strong recruiting center for prestigious Wall Street investment banking firms (such as Goldman, Sachs; JP Morgan; Merrill Lynch; Lehman Brothers; and Morgan Stanley) and leading management consulting firms (such as McKinsey; Bain; Boston Consulting Group; and AT Kearney). Many of my classmates came to Columbia specifically to gain employment with such firms. These firms pay well. Some of my classmates secured starting salaries and bonuses totaling $120,000 or more with these firms. Very lucrative and attractive indeed.

But remember the ROI. These firms gave much, thus also expected a great deal in return. Long hours at the office – regularly working 100 or more hours per week. Constantly being "on-call" – meaning that a person's supervisor could call her into the office to do work, even on Sunday mornings. Dealing with unpleasant clients and stressed-out and egotistical supervisors.

Most people cannot survive for an extended period of time in such difficult environments. The USA Today newspaper recently called these firms, "white collar sweatshops." My classmates at Columbia for the most part knew about what awaited them. Regardless, they wanted to make big money, fast.

Strictly from a professional standpoint, there is a big problem with this idea. Most people leave investment banking or management consulting within two to three years. Unless a person makes enough money during that time to retire, she will have to find another job, probably with companies in traditional industries. These traditional industries do not pay as well as these "white collar sweatshops." There have been situations where a person left investment banking and looked for a job in traditional industries, only to be rebuffed due to her high salary requirement.

Consider the following. Mark is a third year Associate making roughly $200,000 a year. He decides that he has had enough of investment banking and wants to join the finance department of a major drug company. It is likely that Mark would qualify only as a Manager-level or, at best, a Director-level employee. Non-Wall Street companies do not pay Managers or Directors $200,000 annually. Try $75,000 - $125,000. This is about half of what Mark makes at his firm. Companies are hesitant to hire individuals like Mark mainly because of the stark difference in salaries. Essentially, companies fear that if Mark finds a better paying job, he will quit immediately and move on.

Mark, on the other hand, will find quick concern with his new company because there would be a sharp drop in salary and a significant difference in job content. While at the investment bank, he might have had regular interaction with top-level management of client companies, given that he was gaining more experience. However, it is likely that at the traditional company, he will interact mainly with low-to-mid level managers. This is due to the prevalence of entrenched bureaucracies in many traditional firms. This difference in the level of interactions will also result in less strategic and more mundane assignments.

***

Rather than following the investment banking and consulting crowd, I decided that I wanted to find a company where I could develop my career over the long term. A company setting that offered a reasonable salary and a steady pace of development, much like a marathon, appealed to me. Where would I find such companies? In addition, what industry would be best for my future? While considering these questions, I learned my third key lesson from Columbia Business School –

Work for a company that makes technologically innovative products that help people and has a good moral compass.

The first part of this lesson is to find an industry that makes technologically innovative products. I desired technologically innovative products because a steady stream of new innovations within an industry ensures that the industry will last for a long time. Simplistically speaking, innovations bring new product improvements. These produce new market opportunities. New market opportunities result in future revenues. Future revenues ensure future jobs.

The second part of this lesson is to find a technologically innovative industry whose products help people. There are a plethora of technologically innovative industries. But not all help people. Take the defense industry, for example. It is always looking for new technologies. However, their products are not designed to help people on a day-to-day basis.

In my search, I narrowed the candidates down to the pharmaceutical sector and the telecommunications industry. I decided to pursue the pharmaceutical sector because of Mom's illness. I saw how certain drugs made a world of difference in her life. Pharmaceutical companies constantly seek new innovative drugs to bring to market. Plus, for many years, the prescription drug companies have been among the most profitable and financially stable companies in the world. I saw a bright future for me in the pharmaceutical sector.

The third part of this lesson is to find a company that has a good moral compass. I consider myself a person with solid Christian values. I wanted to join a company that exhibited honesty in its business practices and loyalty to its employees, even if it means financial difficulty. I found two drug companies that fit these requirements.

Johnson & Johnson is most famous for its Credo, a statement of corporate values that actively guides Johnson & Johnson's daily business practices. The Credo demands that the company take care of its important responsibilities to its customers, employees, the communities where Johnson & Johnson facilities are located and shareholders. I read numerous articles and books that showed the Credo in action.

The most famous example of Johnson & Johnson's Credo at work was the Tylenol tampering incident of 1982. Some Tylenol products were laced with cyanide, a poisonous substance, and placed back on pharmacy shelves. This led to several deaths. Within a short period of time, Johnson & Johnson decided to eliminate Tylenol from all stores worldwide. Although the company could have just focused on stores in Chicago, it felt that its responsibility was to patients all over the world. As a result, Tylenol disappeared from store shelves until Johnson & Johnson developed new safety seals for its product packaging. Needless to say, Johnson & Johnson lost a great deal of money from this episode. However, Johnson & Johnson thought that it was more important to maintain its reputation and integrity among patients and doctors than to save some money.

I was very impressed. So was Harvard Business School, which wrote a case study that is still used today to teach business students around the world about corporate responsibility and ethical behavior.

Eli Lilly was the other company that impressed me. My research into this company revealed that during the Great Depression, Eli Lilly did not lay off any of its employees. Lilly believed that its greatest assets were not the drugs that it manufactured. Rather, its greatest assets were the people who worked at the company. When the Great Depression occurred in 1929, the country faced many difficulties. This was particularly true of the mid-west. Lilly was and still is based in Indiana. That region of the country is surrounded by agriculture. Lilly was one of the only viable businesses in the region at the time. During the Great Depression, many farms and local businesses faced extreme financial difficulties. Layoffs occurred by the thousands. Social despair was rampant. Lilly resolved not to expose any of its employees to harm. In the face

207

of financial challenges, Lilly weathered the Great Depression and did not lay off any of its employees. I reasoned that if Lilly was concerned about its employees to this extent during such difficult times, how much more would the company do for its employees when the times were good?

I was fixed on these two companies, Johnson & Johnson and Eli Lilly. During the summer between my first and second years at Columbia Business School, I interned at Eli Lilly as a Summer Marketing Associate. I had the opportunity to intern at Johnson & Johnson, but chose Lilly because I had never been to the mid-west. I had been in a large urban setting for too long. I wanted to experience a new environment and a different pace of life.

8. Eli Lilly & Company – Summer Marketing Associate

As a summer intern at Eli Lilly, I worked with the US diabetes marketing team to construct a product lifecycle strategy for an insulin product that had been in the market for a long time. It needed to be retired, in the face of new and improved substitute products that Lilly developed. I found the work extremely invigorating and intellectually stimulating. My background in management consulting and finance came in handy during my project. I introduced analytical techniques that my full-time colleagues had not seen before. I liked my job at Lilly. Lilly liked my output and therefore, invited me to join them for a full-time position after I graduated from Columbia. I was ecstatic!

But reality set in quickly. As it did, I learned two important lessons. My first lesson –

A person should develop her career in a geographic area in proximity to family and friends.

Eli Lilly was a great company with wonderful colleagues. However, it was located in Indianapolis, Indiana. I did not have any family or friends nearby. Also, I was not married. This meant that my only social link to Indianapolis would be Lilly folks. Essentially, outside of Lilly colleagues, I would have no one to count as friends. I would be alone. What if I found my full-time Lilly job to be miserable? I would have no social outlet, except for people who worked at the company. This means that I would not be free to express my views without concern for potential reprisals at work. What if my job was extremely demanding? I would not have opportunities to develop new friendships at church or other social gatherings. I would have no one with whom to enjoy free moments. Also, a person gets older and older, it is more and more difficult to establish new friendships in which she can comfortably reveal her honest feelings. As a result, I began to have serious concerns about going to Indianapolis at this stage of my life.

My second lesson –

A person should join a company located in an area populated with competing companies and other career opportunities.

Lilly was great as a summer internship. But what if it was miserable as a full-time place of employment and I wanted to leave the company? It is pretty much the center of professional opportunity in Indiana.

Where would I find work outside of Lilly? It would have to be outside of Indiana. But how would I pursue opportunities outside of Indiana? I would have to interview, meaning that I would have to use vacation time and other opportunities and travel to other centers of professional opportunity. The large-scale pharmaceutical companies are mostly in the New Jersey and New York areas. Traveling back and forth between Indiana and New York is inconvenient to say the least. I could not risk moving to Indianapolis. I did not want to place such risk on my professional career.

9. *Johnson & Johnson –Manager, Sales & Marketing*

After completing my summer internship at Lilly, I returned to Columbia Business School to complete my MBA. During my second year, I decided that Johnson & Johnson would be a great place to work full-time. With that in mind, I got in contact with my primary recruiter from Johnson & Johnson to express interest in interviewing for a full-time position. As it turned out, Rick considered me "the one that got away." Essentially, he thought that I would have been a fine addition to his department at Johnson & Johnson.

213

Regrettably, I had decided to go elsewhere. Rick assumed that since I had gone to Lilly, I would no longer be interested in Johnson & Johnson. Fortunately, I came back to Johnson & Johnson with an even stronger desire to join the firm than the desire I expressed when I interviewed for a summer internship.

Given the "mutual admiration," my recruiting process was very straight-forward. I received a job offer from Johnson & Johnson in about half the time it took my classmates to get similar job offers from other pharmaceutical companies.

I have been with Johnson & Johnson for the past three years. My first job within was to develop and manage the contracts between the company and a number of important customers of Johnson & Johnson pharmaceutical products as well as medical/surgical equipment. I enjoyed this position because I was exposed to a number of different functional areas within Johnson & Johnson as I developed and managed these contracts. A contract is the encapsulation of all business terms between two business associates. With that, I learned about Johnson & Johnson's most important pharmaceutical and medical/surgical products, what they were, how they were marketed and who were the largest purchasers of these products. This was very much a "down-stream" position – one that entailed a great deal of customer interaction.

Currently, my role is to provide strategic planning input on new pharmaceutical products that are being considered by Johnson & Johnson for the future. It is a more "up-stream" position – one that is more strategy-oriented and entails much less customer interaction.

Thus far, while developing my pharmaceutical industry career at Johnson & Johnson, I have learned three valuable lessons. The first –

Keep a good relationship with all of your colleagues.

You never know when you will interact with someone again in the future and in what capacity. Sanjay was the head of the first department that I joined at Johnson & Johnson. He was my immediate supervisor's boss. With that, he and I only had infrequent business-related discussions. However, during those limited interactions, Sanjay imparted a great deal of knowledge and business acumen to me.

A year after I joined the department, Sanjay moved on to another opportunity and joined a different division of Johnson & Johnson. A year and a half afterwards, I left the same department to join my current department in the pharmaceutical strategic planning division of Johnson & Johnson.

Unbeknownst to me, Sanjay was scheduled to join my new department shortly after I joined. Not only was he going to join my new department, he was going to be my direct supervisor! Needless to say, I was very happy that I was going to work with

216

someone whom I respected and considered a "coach" within Johnson & Johnson. Furthermore, I was relieved that he and I did not have any negative history with one another. This enabled us to come together as a team very quickly and become a highly productive duo in our department.

My second lesson –

Much needed help can come from unexpected sources.

After two years in my first department at Johnson & Johnson, I decided that I needed to take on different challenges and move onto new opportunities within the company. With that in mind, I networked with numerous colleagues throughout the company for advice, leads and introductions to people at departments of interest. Some of these networking efforts were fruitful while some were not.

In the beginning of my search, I focused on my regular business partners within Johnson & Johnson for my networking. I spoke with colleagues with whom I interacted frequently over the past two years. However, I began to realize that I needed to cast a wider net. On a hunch, I contacted Sandip whom I met at a product strategy session nearly two years prior to my job search. He impressed me as an extremely good-hearted and bright person during our first meeting. Perhaps he could provide me with worthwhile advice?

He more than gave me advice. He convinced me that his global pharmaceutical strategic planning department offered the key attributes that I was looking for in my next assignment. Also, Sandip took a liking to my initiative and set up an interview for me with Peter and Paul, the two primary decision makers of the department. Shortly after our meeting, they invited me to join the team. That is how I secured my current job. By the way, Sanjay, my current boss, also got his job because of Sandip's great help.

My third lesson –

Secure your invitation credentials.

In many companies, top executives usually share a certain type of job or credential in common. At Ford, for example, top executives are usually those who developed their careers in the finance department. At Johnson & Johnson, most of the top executives are former sales representatives. Sales reps "carry the bag" which enable them to interact with doctors and learn about how doctors make decisions regarding which products to prescribe to patients or to use with patients. This market knowledge enables them to make the most judicious business decisions about the company's products and strategic decisions. Therefore, sales representative experience is at a premium when it comes to job opportunities in many prestigious departments such as marketing and business development.

Of course, it is not an absolute requirement. There are exceptions to this rule, particularly for those with professional or advanced degrees such as a MD (yes, there are doctors who practice business at Johnson & Johnson, and not medicine), MBA, MA, Ph.D. and MPH (Master of Public Health). My current department predominantly recruits from candidates who possess professional and/or advanced degrees. It literally seems as though every other person has a Ph.D. or a MBA from a prestigious university. The implication is clear. To advance in one's career, a person must be productive in her current role and demonstrate potential for success at the next level. However, the person should also ensure that she has the proper "invitation credentials" such as functional experience and/or academic background so that decision makers will not overlook her candidacy for key promotions.

10. Rutgers Law School – JD Student (Evening Program)

Shortly after joining Johnson & Johnson, I matriculated at Rutgers Law School's evening program in pursuit of my JD degree. After my Lee & Ko experience, I have no intentions to become a practicing attorney. Rather, my logic was that in a heavily regulated industry, such as the pharmaceutical sector, a legal background might come in handy. Besides, Mr. Charles Heimbold, the former Chief Executive Officer of Bristol-Myers Squibb was an attorney during the early days of his career. I'm sure he benefited from his legal acumen at certain points of his pharmaceutical exploits. In addition, in the current dynamic business environment, change is the only constant. Stalwart companies such as Lucent and Enron were here one day and bankrupt the next. This taught me my primary lesson –

Having a spare battery for your career is critical.

What would you do if you found out that your job has been eliminated because of corporate cutbacks? Basically, you need to find another job. Finding a job is not always easy, but having a professional license can facilitate the transition into the job field related to the license.

I learned this from Dad. Although he had a job at Kawasaki, he acquired and maintained a license to drive a taxi in New York City. In case he was laid off, he needed a quick way to find a substitute job. The taxi license would help him to do so. In my case, I am

222

confident that Johnson & Johnson will be around for a long time and I plan to retire from Johnson & Johnson after many years. However, no one knows the future. If for some unfortunate flow of events, Johnson & Johnson folds, I will need a way to continue supporting my family. Being a licensed attorney in NJ will enable me to open up my own legal practice and make sure that my family will not suffer.

11. The Future

As I mentioned above, I intend to stay with Johnson & Johnson throughout my career. I have found an organization that actively cares for its customers, provides generously for its employees, fulfills important civic and community responsibilities and maintains financial strength. I have found a company that makes technologically innovative products that deliver tremendous benefits to society and engages in ethical business practices. My goal is to retire after a long career with Johnson & Johnson.

Johnson & Johnson is not the only company with these admirable attributes. There are many others waiting to be found. The next chapter is designed to assist the reader in identifying career opportunities that are just as rewarding.

V. How to Select an Ideal Career

Paul J. Kim

1. When should a person begin to think about careers and industries?

The most important aspect about selecting a career is to begin considering future career interests earlier in one's development.

If I had to do it all over, I would have begun to place serious thought towards my career interests while in high school.

This is critical because this would have impacted where I would have applied for college and what I would have studied. I have, on occasion, heard from

Johnson & Johnson colleagues that if they knew that they would have been working for Johnson & Johnson, they would have studied biology and marketing while in college.

A career decision made in high school may seem to be premature. However, it does provide strong focus for one's activities while applying to college and once in college. A person can change her mind regarding career paths several times before finding the right one. In order to make the transition from one to another, a person needs readily transferable skills. It is more likely that a person will have developed marketable skills if a person was focused and meaningfully pursuing a certain career path than if she was indecisive and meandering amongst career fields for an extended period of time.

2. How can a person learn about different careers and industries?

While it is key to begin considering different career paths early, it is even more critical to consider different career paths under the guidance of those already traversing those paths.

These individuals are the alumni of a person's school who are in different career paths.

Schools regularly maintain lists of alumni, organized by different careers and industries. The

Paul J. Kim

Stuyvesant High School Alumni Association produces a list of all alumni once every five years and provides information on what each alumnus does for a living and how to get in touch with these individuals. Among the alumni, there are doctors, lawyers, engineers, police officers, publishers, astronauts, chemists, political activities, legislators, research scientists and investment bankers.

In general, alumni welcome calls from students eager to learn about different career paths.

Also, people like to talk about themselves and are interested in opportunities to do so. Some may even invite a student to spend the day with them at their place of employment to see first-hand what it is like to be . . . let's say a psychiatrist or a toxicologist for a petroleum company.

By the way, when I was a student at Columbia Business School and considering Eli Lilly and Johnson

& Johnson, I spent hours speaking with alumni at these companies to see if what I read about these companies was in fact true. My high level of interest in these companies, evidenced by my phone calls and probing questions, had a positive impact on my recruiting efforts with them. The alumni were usually involved (directly or indirectly) with the on-campus recruiting efforts of their respective companies at Columbia Business School. Consequently, I secured internships with both Eli Lilly and Johnson & Johnson before my classmates even began interviewing with these companies for summer jobs.

An effective way to learn about different industries is to read weekly business magazines and daily business-related newspapers.

The focus of these periodicals is to discuss what is happening in the business world – who the players are, what they are doing now and in the future and how this will impact the future. By reading these business journals, a person will gain a good understanding of what types of industries (whether aerospace, pharmaceutical, retail, etc.) produce technologically innovative and financially rewarding goods that provide meaningful benefits to society through ethical business practices.

Other sources of great information include the following.

First, national business magazines annually publish lists of the leading companies throughout the world.

These companies are also listed by the different industries in which they do business. I benefited from these lists because they identified all of the major pharmaceutical and telecommunications companies for me. They provided me with an inventory of target companies to engage while looking for a job.

Second, there are fantastic job search websites as well as career review websites that provide a close up look at different industries and different companies.

These websites usually conduct numerous interviews with people working in different industries and companies. With their immense amount of information, they regularly produce extremely helpful overviews.

Third, books have been published on various career paths that are suitable for those with different academic backgrounds. They provide an enlightening look at different career trajectories.

These were the books that I wish I had when I was in high school!! They not only describe various careers, they identify the type of education required to enter each field, what type of careers are suited for different personalities and provide tips on how to secure good jobs. A definite must-read.

3. How should a person select a future career?

As I mentioned above, I selected the pharmaceutical industry because I was looking for an industry that made technologically innovative products that provided benefits to society. I selected Johnson & Johnson because I wanted a company that had a good moral compass. Furthermore, I selected strategic marketing as my functional area of expertise because I was academically trained for it (I majored in marketing while at Columbia Business School) and because I had practical work experience in that area (as a management consultant with Bain & Company).

The caveat is the following. Everyone selects a career for unique reasons. This is because everyone has distinct values and interprets those values differently when analyzing industries and companies. Essentially, the analytical method that worked for me may not work for someone else.

The key, however, is to identify one's own value system and apply it to one's career selection. If a person's career is not in line with her values, that person will eventually become unhappy and most likely seek out another career.

For example, I valued my time spent with family and friends. Therefore, I wanted a career that would afford me a good balance between personal and work time. This is one of the biggest reasons why I decided against returning to management consulting after graduating from Columbia.

Understand your values and let them guide you to a career path that provides you with what you want out of your professional life.

Paul J. Kim

VI. Closing Thoughts

Paul J. Kim

1. Now that you have read this book . . . .

By any measure, admission to a competitive college is an indication that an individual demonstrated a meaningful level of dedication to her academic, extracurricular and personal responsibilities during high school. The student has built a strong personal momentum to reach the next level up in one's development.

However, attending a competitive college is not a guarantee of future personal or professional success.

While in college, the student should continue with the level of dedication and hard work that characterized her high school years.

As the former high school student, now a college student, strives to reach the next level of her development after college (whether it is graduate school, law school or medical school, or a certain type of professional position), attending a competitive undergraduate institution is like being given a pass to ride the escalator while attending a non-competitive college is like having to climb the stairs. The escalator will make her climb to the next level a bit easier than taking the stairs. Nevertheless, if she just stands still on the escalator, she will reach the next level almost at the same time as a person diligently climbing up the staircase. The wise person on the escalator will climb up step-by-step while on the escalator in order to get to the next level all-the-more faster.

Indeed, attending a competitive college provides an opportunity for an individual to maximize on the personal momentum she developed during high school and to transform that momentum into an all-the-more rewarding post-college pursuit, whether this pursuit is to further one's education or to embark upon a future career. However, the key is for the student to recognize and take advantage of this opportunity by maintaining the strong effort she developed in high school throughout her college years.

Maintaining that momentum requires having a post-graduation goal to strive for once in college. As any sailor will concur, without a rudder, a boat will go in many different and often unproductive directions.

Having a goal will optimize a person's college experience by guiding her selection of academic discipline, extracurricular activities, part-time jobs and summer pursuits so that these will increase the likelihood that the person will attain the goal.

Throughout this book, I have shared my efforts in high school that produced an admission to Harvard. But more importantly, I have shared my challenges and lessons during and after Harvard that helped me to construct my current successful professional career. I hope that by reading about my experiences before, during and after the college of my dreams, all readers will learn from my mistakes and triumphs, but more importantly, develop and carry out their own plans for prosperity.

***

Lastly, for nearly a decade, I have served as a consultant specializing in college and business school admissions as well as career development strategies. Together, my clients and I have tackled these three key issues:

How to get into a competitive college or business school;

How to use one's time wisely while at a competitive college or business school; and

How to develop one's long-term career upon graduating from a prestigious university.

If you would like more information about private consulting services or group seminars, please contact me at: pauljkim@post.harvard.edu

Paul J. Kim

About the Author

Paul J. Kim grew up in Flushing, NY and attended the highly selective Stuyvesant High School in Manhattan. He then earned a Bachelor of Arts degree with honors from Harvard University and a Master of Business Administration degree from Columbia Business School. He has served as an alumni admissions interviewer for these two Ivy League institutions over the past decade.

Mr. Kim is currently a global strategic planner with the pharmaceutical division of Johnson & Johnson, a worldwide healthcare industry conglomerate. His previous career milestones include international management consulting and Wall Street finance. In his spare time, he is a consultant specializing in college/business school admissions and career development strategies.

Mr. Kim resides in suburban New Jersey with his wife Yuni.

Printed in the United States
1506400001B/187